M000316772

Endorsements

Having experienced two moves of God, the revival called the Jesus Movement in which I was called to the ministry and the revival that broke out in Toronto when I went there to preach, and having been in hotspots for revival in Argentina, Brazil, Russia, Ukraine, and Mozambique, I am a man excited by the heartbeat of revival. I love the electricity in the air of expectant faith for what God is going to do. The testimonies of divine appointments, healings, and deliverances which are more common in times of revival excite me, filling me with joy for the advancement of God's Kingdom. When I read Jessi Green's *Wildfires: A Field Guide to Supernatural Revival*, I was greatly encouraged. I found her story of her personal pilgrimage and that of her husband's to be engaging and encouraging. As I approach the sunset score of my life, it is so encouraging to see the sovereign God raising up new revivalists who burn with His passion for souls and the awakening of His body, the Church, out of its slumber. Jessi burns with personal fire from God. She, a millennial, has written a most encouraging book giving us hope, not that revival is coming, but that revival has already begun again. Revivals historically have always been occurring for several years before the public notes what God is doing. I encourage you to buy and read *Wildfires*, in doing so, you will be seeding your own spirit with the seeds of revival.

—**Randy Clark**
D.D., D.Min., Th.D., M.Div., B.S. Religious Studies
Overseer of the apostolic network of Global Awakening
President of Global Awakening Theological Seminary

There are so many reasons why I love this book! *Wildfires* is honest, raw, and passionately focused on Jesus, the person of revival. I can't imagine anyone reading this book and not burning in their hearts for more—more of all that Jesus intends to do in and through His people. This book is unique because author, Jessi Green, has written this book in the midst of revival. Each page tells the challenging and often vulnerable process of yielding her life to pursue one vision: the Kingdom of God invading the state of California. When truth moves from a concept to conviction, it dramatically affects behavior. In *Wildfires*, Jessi gives us a present-day account of both the struggles and the breakthroughs that come with stewarding a move of God. Each page carries valuable insight for navigating our current moment with the Holy Spirit. God is truly on the move, and we owe Him the absolute abandonment of our "yes."

—**Bill Johnson**
Bethel Church, Redding, CA
Author of *The Way of Life and Born for Significance*

Wildfires by Jessi Green is a challenging, raw appeal for you and me to go all in for Jesus. To see the promised revival and harvest break out all over North America and the world. Her transparent life stories will grip and challenge any hidden, unacknowledged complacency. Jessi confronts you with challenging faith in action that is dangerously contagious.

I am desperate for revival myself, and I could hardly put her book down.

—**John Arnott**
Catch the Fire, Toronto
Author of *Preparing for the Glory*

"What would your life look like if you were fully alive?" The question Jessi Green presents at the beginning of this book will provoke you. I find *Wildfires* captivating, compelling, and a book that has the ability to transform society. And boy, do we need it! The timing in history of the release of this book is amazing! Jessi left a lifestyle of what looked from the outside like "having it all together," but she was hardly living. She found Jesus and came to know what living a radical lifestyle for Him could look like—and she became alive on the inside again! Jessi's passion to see souls saved for the Kingdom of God is contagious! Everyone needs this book, and personally, I'm going to pick up a copy for every member of my ministry team!

—**Ana Werner**
Founder of Ana Werner Ministries
President, Eagles Network
Author and prophetic seer
www.anawerner.org

Jessi is just herself in this book. That's why this read is so fresh, non-plastic, and organic. Follow her on a wild and transparent ride into the heart of God. You'll be challenged to settle for nothing less than the abundant life Jesus promised to give.

—**Bob Sorge**
Author, *Secrets of the Secret Place*

My heart burned while reading *Wildfires*. The rawness and purity of Jessi's heart is so refreshing. If you weren't hungry for Jesus when you opened the pages, you certainly will be by the end.

Revival is sovereign, the Kingdom has a culture, discipleship is costly, and God wants to use you in it all. This book will take you by the hand

and help you walk out the process to be used by God and have your Kingdom dreams fulfilled. Take it from me, this book will fuel the fire inside your heart.

—**Elizabeth Tiam-Fook**
International Young Prophets
Maricopa, Arizona

Revival is not something that God sends but something His believers become. I believe this book will awaken people to the truth of the Gospel, and the outcome will be a lifestyle that results in revival.

—**Dylan Long**
Awakening Europe
Outreach Coordinate

Being friends with Jessi in the midst of her stepping out in faith against all odds during one of the most turbulent times our nation has ever seen, was both inspiring and challenging. Her radical devotion to simply love Jesus and do whatever He said no matter what the cost, stirred my own faith, even to the point of jumping into the baptismal tank at the tent meeting to be all in once again. Let me tell you right now, getting to know Jessi is anything but comfortable. But I think once we really get to know Jesus, we will find the same thing is true with Him. Once we lock eyes with His, we will be inspired to throw off everything that hinders and run the race set before us with total abandonment. Jessi's relationship with Jesus will compel you to do the same. In *Wildfires*, Jessi brings her whole heart and extends her hand to invite you into her story. She then leads you deeper into the burning heart of God. *Wildfires* in not for the faint-hearted. But if you are courageous enough to go on this journey with Jessi, you will come out the other side a burning one for Jesus, guaranteed. As you read *Wildfires*, may you be marked by God's consuming fire to the point of no return.

—**Jennifer A. Miskov, Ph.D.**
Revival historian
Founding Director of School of Revival and Writing in the Glory

I have watched Jessi Green over the last decade lead her generation to seek after God. She describes herself as being "wildly passionate," and that passion is evident on every page of her book. If you sense that there is more to your walk with God and are looking for the spark to light a fire in your life, *Wildfires* is the book you need!

—**Seth Barnes**
Founder and executive director
Adventures in Missions and The World Race

Jessi is one of those new breed of fiery revivalists who is first and foremost totally in love with Jesus and lives to follow and obey Him in the fear of the Lord. She knows what it means to do what Jesus said—to take up her cross and follow Him. Nothing is counted as loss to her in making Jesus known and giving her life for those who have never known this great love.

Jessi through her own story shows us the reward of losing her life, yielding, and finding it in Jesus Christ. To not only hear the voice of the Lord but to act even at great cost to herself personally, her family, and her reputation. She is a voice calling a generation to be surrendered and devoted wholly to Jesus and to live a life of no compromise. To be all in and to be set on fire by the love of God, to be revival for the rest of our lives!

—**Kate Smith**
President, Catch the Fire World

Jessi Green takes us on a wild ride that catapults into the heart of the Father and His aim for true worshipers to go out into the harvest, no matter the cost and no matter the opposition.

I have seen her stand with Jesus on beaches in Southern California and Santa Cruz and find those who need a message of hope in the darkness. If you are looking for a book to awaken you to find your calling as a Christian, look no further. I was mesmerized and you will be too!

—Theresa Dedmon
Author, *Born to Create and Created To Overcome: An Interactive Journey of the Heart through Art and Poetry*
Pastor, artist, speaker, creative catalyst, founder of Create Academy
Theresadedmon.com

I remember it so clearly: my colleagues and I were with author and revival leader, Dr. Michael Brown, in his office, praying for revival. It was a different kind of prayer. Tears were released and there was a groan in the spirit—a desperate cry for a new generation of revivalists to come forth in the power of the Spirit, preaching the Truth of the Gospel. Very shortly after this meeting, through sovereign orchestration, I got to meet Jessi and Parker Green in California. There was not talk of a book deal; there were only more tears spontaneously shed as we had breakfast together in Huntington Beach, talking about what the Spirit of the Lord was doing up and down the coast of California. Since then, we've become fast friends and co-laborers in revival. This book will completely dismantle the lie of "revival is coming one day, some day." The move of God is available now to whosoever would say "YES." That's the testimony of Jessi Green and the power of *Wildfires*. This book will ignite your faith to never settle, never back down, and never embrace any sub-standard, non-Biblical version of Christianity again. It will effectively ruin you in all the right ways. Why? Jessi is not a celebrity preacher. She is not out to build a name or a platform. She is a wife, a mother, and a Jesus-follower who gave the Spirit of God a complete and costly "Yes." *Wildfires* reveals the supernatural lifestyle that's possible to any believer who gives King Jesus a complete YES!

—**Larry Sparks, MDiv.**
Publisher, Destiny Image
lawrencesparks.com

Jessi Green is one of the most authentic believers and leaders I have observed in the Body of Christ. In her book *Wildfires*, you will receive an invitation and strong exhortation to engage in revival, to live an uncompromised life, to be filled with JESUS—His heart and His passion, and to live in complete abandonment. Jessi brings you inside of her journey…her heart. *Wildfires* is sure to set a fire within you—your light belongs in the darkness. You were called for such a time as this.

—**Patricia King**
Author, minister, television host

Jessi's passion for Jesus and people is reflected on every page of her book *Wildfires*. I am certain that as you read there will be an impartation and transfer of this very needed passion. Her personal story, coupled with the experience of leading a significant revival and outpouring will inspire, challenge, and compel you to believe for all that God has for you and all that He can do through you. Thank you, Jessi, for returning us to the core of our Christianity, passion for Jesus, and passion for people.

—**Pastor Kim Owens**
Co-lead pastor of Fresh Start Church, Peoria, AZ
Author of *Doorkeepers of Revival*

We must operate in the anointing of the Holy Spirit, in His baptism without the religious dead works. This book offers keys for us to be set ablaze with an anointing from the throne room of Heaven, to be washed clean in the bridegroom's blood, and to be empowered by the Holy Ghost. *Wildfires* is a book that is right from the heart of Father God; it is laced with purity and wisdom. Read it today and you will be set free to flourish in your true calling.

—**Sarah Glover**
Australian Wild Chef
Author of *Wild Adventure Cookbook*

When I heard what God was doing in Southern California, my heart was stirred with fire. I had read books that were written years ago about a Jesus people movement and how thousands of young people were flocking to the ocean to be baptized and follow Jesus. There is a wildfire of revival that God is stirring in the hearts of the young and old. The stage has been set. God is calling out to man and man is calling out to God to have God disturb the normal. The word of the Lord has been sent out and it is taking root in the soil of humble hearts. As you read through the pages of *Wildfires,* my prayer is that you would find yourself on your knees in prayer and worship.

I pray that this book will light a fire in you to go into your room, shut the door and say "Holy Spirit come and visit me." May this book be a tool to light the fire in you to touch a generation with the raw power of God.

—**Chris Overstreet**
Evangelist
Compassion to Action

Jessi Green's book *Wildfires* is a handbook for the hour. In this era of incredible outpouring of His Spirit and time of revival, this book will ignite hunger and passion within you for Jesus. It will call you to the front line, prepare you, and position you for what is the greatest move of the Spirit of God in the earth that we have ever seen. This book carries a weighty anointing to awaken you and call you into the place of living FULLY alive—a place that is yours in Christ (John 10:10). It will help you break free from any complacency or apathy. These are pages of purity that will ignite the first love fire deeper within you. What a gift this book is!

—**Lana Vawser**
Lana Vawser Ministries

Wildfires is the ultimate invitation to awaken your soul and step into your true calling as a Christian; in this very moment! Jessi's passion and fire for the Lord is the very heart of revival in this world and is calling us all to take part in what God is doing. *Wildfires* is a necessary guide for everyone who wants to revolt against apathy and start walking boldly in faith.

—**Desiree Siegfried**
The Bachelorette 9
Host of *Heart of Purpose* Podcast
Desiree Hartsock Bridal

Prepare for a touch from the Holy Spirit as you delve into this handbook on authentic revival. Jessi taps into the Father's heart for His Bride as she shares her testimony in a refreshingly raw way. Stunning, from beginning to end!

—**Elizabeth Johnston**
Bestselling author, speaker, & mom of 10

wildfires

**A FIELD GUIDE
TO SUPERNATURAL REVIVAL**

*Revolt against apathy
& (ignite) the world
with God's Power!*

JESSI GREEN

© Copyright 2021–Jessi Green

All rights reserved. This book is protected by the copyright laws of the United States of America. This book may not be copied or reprinted for commercial gain or profit. The use of short quotations or occasional page copying for personal or group study is permitted and encouraged. Permission will be granted upon request. Unless otherwise identified, Scripture quotations are taken from the HOLY BIBLE, NEW INTERNATIONAL VERSION®, Copyright © 1973, 1978, 1984, 2011 International Bible Society. Used by permission of Zondervan. All rights reserved. Scripture quotations marked NLT are taken from the Holy Bible, New Living Translation, copyright 1996, 2004, 2015. Used by permission of Tyndale House Publishers, Wheaton, Illinois 60189. All rights reserved. Scripture quotations marked NKJV are taken from the New King James Version. Copyright © 1982 by Thomas Nelson, Inc. Used by permission. All rights reserved. Scripture quotations marked TPT are taken from The Passion Translation, Copyright © 2014, 2015, 2016, 2017, www.thepassiontranslation. com. Used by permission of BroadStreet Publishing Group, LLC, Racine, Wisconsin, USA. All rights reserved. Scripture quotations marked NASB are taken from the NEW AMERI-CAN STANDARD BIBLE®, Copyright © 1960, 1962, 1963, 1968, 1971, 1972, 1973, 1975, 1977, 1995 by The Lockman Foundation. Used by permission. Scripture quotations marked AMP are taken from the Amplified® Bible, Copyright © 2015 by The Lockman Foundation, La Habra, CA 90631. All rights reserved. Used by permission. Scripture quotations marked KJV are taken from the King James Version. Scripture quotations marked ESV are taken from The Holy Bible, English Standard Version® (ESV®), copyright © 2001 by Crossway, a pub-lishing ministry of Good News Publishers. Used by permission. All rights reserved. Scripture quotations marked MSG are taken from The Message. Copyright © 1993, 1994, 1995, 1996, 2000, 2001, 2002. Used by permission of NavPress Publishing Group. Scripture quotations marked ISV are taken from the International Standard Version® Copyright © 1996-2008 by the ISV Foundation. Used by permission of Davidson Press. All rights reserved internation-ally. All emphasis within Scripture quotations is the author's own. Please note that Destiny Image's publishing style capitalizes certain pronouns in Scripture that refer to the Father, Son, and Holy Spirit, and may differ from some publishers' styles. Take note that the name satan and related names are not capitalized. We choose not to acknowledge him, even to the point of violating grammatical rules.

DESTINY IMAGE® PUBLISHERS, INC.

P.O. Box 310, Shippensburg, PA 17257-0310

"Promoting Inspired Lives."

This book and all other Destiny Image and Destiny Image Fiction books are available at Chris-tian bookstores and distributors worldwide.

Cover design by Christian Rafetto

For more information on foreign distributors, call 717-532-3040.

Reach us on the Internet: www.destinyimage.com.

ISBN 13 TP: 978-0-7684-5927-2

ISBN 13 eBook: 978-0-7684-5928-9

ISBN 13 HC: 978-0-7684-5930-2

ISBN 13 LP: 978-0-7684-5929-6

For Worldwide Distribution, Printed in the U.S.A.

4 5 6 7 8 / 25 24 23 22 21

Dedication

I dedicate this book to my daughter,
Summer Kingsley Green.
I birthed you, while birthing **revival.**
I nursed you under the tent,
while people rushed into the Pacific Ocean
to be baptized and follow Jesus.
I always knew I'd have a daughter named Summer.
Summer in Latin is the word **Aestas,** which means
"burn; fire."
Fire is symbolic of anointing, being holy, set apart, pure.
We burn with the flame of God because
it is evidence of His presence in us.
This is my letter to you; may you find **hope** in its pages.

This could be the year of revival...

There seems to be a notion abroad that if we talk enough and pray enough, revival will set in like a stock market boom or a winning streak on a baseball club. We appear to be waiting for some sweet chariot to swing low and carry us into the Big Rock Candy Mountain of religious experience.

Well, it is a pretty good rule that if everyone is saying something it is not likely to be true; or, if it has truth at the bottom, it has been so distorted by wrong emphasis as to have the effect of error in its practical outworking. And such, I believe, is much of the revival talk we hear today.

My reason for doubt of the soundness of it is that we appear to conceive of revival as a kind of benign miracle, a feverish renaissance of religious activity which will come upon us, leaving us morally just as we are now, except that we will be a lot happier and there will be a great many more of us. It's a good talking point and it has an aura of superior godliness about it; but the trouble is that it is just not true.

Our mistake is that we want God to send revival on our terms. We want to get the power of God into our hands, to call it to us that it may work for us in promoting and furthering our kind of Christianity. We want still to be in charge, guiding the chariot through the religious sky in the direction we want it to go, shouting Glory to God, it is true, but modestly accepting a share of the glory for ourselves in a nice inoffensive sort of way. We are calling on God to send fire on our altars, completely ignoring the fact that they are our altars and not God's. And like the prophets of Baal we are working ourselves into a frenzy as if we could by violence command the arm of the Almighty.

The whole error results from a confused notion of revival and a failure to recognize the moral laws that underlie the Kingdom of God. God never moves whimsically; His ways are never impulsive or erratic. He never sends judgment unless there has been a violation of His laws, nor does He send blessing apart from obedience to those laws. So precise are His movements both in justice and in mercy that an intelligent observer, aware of the circumstances, could predict with complete accuracy any visitation of judgment or grace God might send to a nation, a church or an individual.

Of this we may be certain: We cannot continue to ignore God's will as expressed in the Scriptures and expect to secure the aid of God's Spirit. God has given us a complete blueprint for the Church and He requires that we adhere to it 100 percent. Message, morals ,and methods are there, and we are under strict obligation to be faithful to all three.

Today we have the strange phenomenon of a company of Christians solemnly protesting to heaven and earth the purity of their Bible creed, and at the same time following the unregenerate world in their methods and managing only with difficulty to keep their moral standards from sinking out of sight. Coldness, worldliness, pride, boasting, lying, misrepresenting, love of money, exhibitionism—all these things are practiced by professedly orthodox Christians, not in secret but in plain sight and often as a necessary part of the whole religious show.

It will take more than talk and prayer to bring revival. There must be a return to the Lord in practice before our prayers will be heard in heaven.

—**A. W. Tozer,** *The Size of the Soul*

Contents

Foreword

*When the Lord restored the fortunes of Zion we were like
those who dream, then our mouth was filled with laughter and
our tongue with the shouts of joy. Then they said among the
nations, "The Lord has done great things for them." The Lord
has done great things for us, and we are glad. Bring back our
captivity, Oh Lord, as the streams in the South. Those who sow
in tears will reap in joy. He who continually goes forth weeping,
bearing seed for sowing, shall doubtless come again with
rejoicing, bringing his sheaves with him.*
—Psalm 126 ESV

For many of us who lived in the '70s, streams in the south (South-ern California) is what we experienced. These were the days of the Jesus movement. We were like those who dreamed. Streams of the Holy Spirit were flowing. Thousands were being saved and being baptized in the ocean or in swimming pools or bathtubs. We were sing-ing, "just get me down to the river." Oh the simplicity of it all. You could have said boo and people would be saved. "Little Pilgrim[s] walking down the road of life" did "lend an ear to a love song" and for so many "one way" became the only way. We were one in spirit we were one in the Lord.

While the high waters of the Woodstock hippy revolution of the '60s were drying up and songs of joy turned to questioning, "Where have all the flowers gone?" I stepped into a living room afterglow service where they were singing in the Spirit and the flowers of my soul blossomed. It was like my spirit flew to heaven and I drank from the river of His pleasures. A few days later I was shouting, "I'm saved! I'm saved!" I bought all the gospels of John, went into the mall to share Jesus, was kicked out of the mall, preached in the movie theater. So many young leaders were likewise being called out of formal religion into a love-induced, "follow the voice," spontaneous, courageous obedience. It was government by the Spirit. It was like that THEN.

But THEN went away and for many, the dream faded and the church was singing, "Where have all the flowers gone?" WHEN became our longing cry. WHEN will you revive us again? And THEN in the '80s God gave us back our vineyards and healing waters flowed and we sang as we sang in the days of our youth. It was like that THEN. But THEN became WHEN again. THEN in the '90s God poured out the Father's blessing and literally our mouths were filled with laughter and our tongues with shouts of joy! It was like that THEN.

Yet for years now many have been longing for the days of the love, simplicity, and widespread evangelism of the Jesus movement again. With weeping they have been sowing their seeds, crying out to God to restore our fortunes like streams in the desert and bring in the harvest ...THEN suddenly!...

...WILDFIRES! This book in your hands!...oh my gosh! It's the dream! Streams in the South! Spirit saturating Orange County! Hundreds being saved, baptized on the beaches of Southern California. It's out of the buildings and onto the beaches. Healings out in the open, God coming out of hiding. The book is a story and much more, a prophecy, a harbinger of great things to come. It's a roar, "Do not say there is yet four months to the harvest, lift up your eyes, the fields are ripe for harvest!"

But *Wildfires* is not just testimonies of evangelism and revival. It's the cost, the agony of preparation. It's the hammer of truth. It's not just searching the Bible but the Bible searching you. Paul Bilheimer wrote, "When God wants to use a man and fuse a man how he hammers him and hurts him, and with mighty blows converts him, God knows what he's about." In this book, it's about when God wants to use and fuse a woman. It's the story of Jessi Green and her fasting, praying husband Parker. It's about the deep root and rugged route that leads to the amazing fruit of revival.

Like the counterculture of the '60s prepared the way for the Jesus movement and a new breed of leaders like Keith and Melody Green, so too the crushing Covid, antichrist, and cancel cultures of 2020 have prepared the way for another Green family and a new breed of radical evangelists and leaders who will not be confined by fear and fatalism. Theirs is the anthem, "We must obey God rather than man." The Greens' story is like an act taken out of Acts. No Hollywood fluff here. It's a call to sacrifice and consecration, purity, and devotion, a legacy of Keith Green no compromise. It's a "Sell all, Leave all, Risk all, Reach all" reality. Forged out of fasting and "pound it out in prayer" crucibles, the Green's New Deal is shifting the climate in Southern California to revival land. Their story is daring drama leading to humble confrontation with California's silencing systems and watching last-minute rescue operations from heaven. It's all about souls! souls! souls! It's all about Jesus!

My prayer is that this book will provoke a new generation of revivalists who are not content with good meetings but who are willing to grind revival out on the anvil of deep consecration and ridiculous faith so that something comes to earth of which it can truly be said, "It came down out of heaven."

Are we in a new Jesus movement? We will soon see, but in reading this book I'm beginning to be like those who dream. A friend of mine in the days of the Jesus movement asked some bystanders, "What time is it?" With simplicity and wildness, they responded, "It's time for you to get saved!" And he did. What time is it? Read this book. It may be telling us, "It's time for the church, in the words of the old hymn, to be 'Bringing in the sheaves, bringing in the sheaves,' then 'We shall come rejoicing bringing in the sheaves.'"

—Lou Engle
co-founder of TheCall

Introduction

During the summer of 2020, my husband Parker and I had the opportunity to begin leading revival on the beaches of Orange County, California. I use the word *revival* with care and caution. To be honest, I think it can be one of the most misused and often abused words in Christian culture. I've learned quickly that revival is way more than a Christian conference. It is the Church, the saints, being awakened, revived, and set ablaze with the Kingdom of God. What was ignited in the summer of 2020 is extremely significant for the new ground being laid out for the Church in this hour. As my husband and I step into leading revival in new cities, in tents, and on the streets, I can't help but notice that this moment is an opportunity for all of us.

Throughout history, we see times when God has truly poured out His Spirit and transformed entire regions with His glory. I believe revival isn't just a sovereign act of God, but the Holy Spirit is searching for consecrated burning ones who want Him above all things. I am wildly excited to share more about this with you as we begin this journey together.

On a daily basis, I whisper to myself, "This can't all really be happening, can it?" I fondly remember my first few winters evangelizing in New

York City in my mid-20s. At the time, I wasn't being invited to preach anywhere. I was desperately searching for resources on how to share the Gospel, and I felt a bit lost myself. There were so many cold afternoons when I would stop someone on the street and ask, "What does the word *freedom* mean to you?" This was my desperate conversation opener for a chance to stop the blur of the city to share the Gospel with a stranger.

I remember the first time my street evangelism methods "worked." I was in a small deli and asked a woman in her mid-50s my little "freedom question." She quietly responded, and for a moment I was lit up with the fact that we were actually having a conversation and not distracted by the busy world around us. While she waited for her egg sandwich, I probed further. As my heart raced and my fingers trembled, I muttered out, "Is there anything I can pray for you about?"

She said, "Yes."

As I prayed for her finances, I felt like I was diving into the deep end of my small faith and wasn't sure if I knew how to swim. As we prayed, I begged God to show up and do something. I looked the woman in the eyes and asked her, "Do you feel God's presence right now?"

She looked at me, shocked, and said, "Yes, yes I do."

I was equally shocked.

I then grabbed her cold, weather-beaten hands in mine and shared the Gospel with her in a whisper. "Jesus loves you. He really loves you, and He is really real! He wants to forgive you for your sins. He died on the cross for your sins and rose from the dead! Jesus is alive and wants to give you a brand-new life! Do you want that brand-new life? Do you want to follow Jesus?"

She said, "Yes!"

I couldn't believe it. I felt the ecstatic emotion of Christmas morning burning in my chest. An uncontainable joy consumed me and I began to cry as I held her in my arms. Then we prayed together. Among the old coffee machines, construction workers in line for breakfast, and steam floating in the air from the hot griddle, she was saved. She was saved in that deli on 23rd Street!

It was a simple, ordinary day in an ordinary place, but I immediately became addicted to sharing the Gospel. I learned a lifetime lesson in that moment: You don't need to be famous, you don't need great lights and music, you don't need to be in a special place or need permission to be used by God.

Evangelist Smith Wigglesworth once said, "The Acts of the Apostles was written because the apostles acted!"

Since that day at the deli, I have been in acceleration mode when it comes to sharing the Gospel. I have had the opportunity to learn from some of the world's greatest evangelists (including the late Reinhard Bonnke), pick up new tools from some of the most creative missionaries on earth, step out in faith in wild ways, fail miserably, have an identity crisis, surrender everything, overcome fear, read piles of books, practice what those books say, surrender everything again, plant micro churches, make disciples in my living room, and lead thousands upon thousands into eternal life through Jesus Christ!

I believe that we are in revival. Now. Like, *today*.

In the pages that follow, I will invite you into the story of a revival that is happening now. We will also glean from revivalists of the past to define misused terms on this subject.

In Matthew 9:37-38 Jesus said to His disciples, "The harvest is plentiful but the workers are few. Ask the Lord of the harvest, therefore, to send out workers into his harvest field."

Perhaps Jesus is sending us out, *you* and I, together.

I promise on these pages to be as vulnerable with you as I possibly can. I pray that we learn to trust one another, that we would become kin, family that goes forth into battle with one heart and one mind. I hope this field guide helps you along the way. I pray that the lessons I learned that came at a great cost would help you overcome every snare and trap of the enemy. Keep it close, share it with your dearest friends, and, together, let's sustain a never-ending flame of revival till the return of King Jesus.

Dearest Kin,

My heart is on fire, boiling over w/ passion. Bubbling up within me are these beautiful lyrics as a lovely poem to be sung for the King. Like a river bursting its banks, I'm Overflowing w/ words, spilling out into this sacred story. (Psalm 45:1 TPT)

Here we go!!

This journey begins just like every other tale. Its the original story. The one written for each of us since the Beginning of Time.

"There has to be more..."

Oh, how our souls have longed to satisfy the insatiable quest that nags us. The reality is, there <u>is</u> <u>more</u> — so much more !!!...

We were created, designed, and orchestrated to experience life. A raging fire of explosive LIFE is in the Distance. When we draw closer, we can *feel* the warmth of the fire. The world convinces us "Thats enough, Dont press in further. The fire... its Dangerous!"

So —
we set up camps — miles away. We settle on watching the flames but neglect to be invited / ignited.

_____ We sit on our computers, work long hours to accumulate more status, more resources, More,

More,

More of (Anything) that can give us the temporal feeling of the ~~flames~~. Slowly → we start to put our head down, growing wearily [Apathetic]. We believe the LIE that the abundant Kingdom LIFE is for some other fortunate soul

I PLEAD YOU, DON'T GIVE UP SO EASILY!!

Your workplace should be ignited w/ color. You should go to sleep EXPECTANT to * dream * and hear from the Creator of the Universe.

You see, this book is a journey into Revival. No, not a bunch of "Christian Hype," but Actual Revival.

Revival that looks like a treasure in a field, ~~that once~~ you discover it you'd be willing to lay (everything) down for it.

I WISH I could KNEEL down in front of you
And put your hands into my charcoaled palms,
And whisper into your EAR,
"It's not coming,
It's here.
The FIRE is Here. Can you Feel its heat.
It's time to go in."
Will it cost you?
Well, yeah ... of course.
Everything with value does.
But.... we both know what you have been
doing isn't working. So, WHY Not Just go
ALL IN AND SEE WHAt happens WHEN
you allow the flames of His holy fire to
consume you?
His love is An All-consuming FiRE.

Lets go
Jessie

[YAy!! I'm so EXciteD!!]

Song of Solomon
8:6-7 (TPT)

Fasten me upon your heart as a seal of fire forevermore.
This living, consuming flame
will seal you as my prisoner of love.
My passion is stronger
than the chains of death and the grave,
all consuming as the very flashes of fire
from the burning heart of God.
Place this fierce, unrelenting fire over your entire being.
Rivers of pain and persecution
will never extinguish this flame.
Endless floods will be unable
to quench this raging fire that burns within you.
Everything will be consumed.
It will stop at nothing
as you yield everything to this furious fire
until it won't even seem to you like a sacrifice anymore.

PART 1

Wildfire

*The reports about Jesus spread like **wildfire** throughout every community in the surrounding region.*

—Luke 4:37 TPT

CHAPTER 1

Are You Really Living?

*So many of us
are starving for life
and have no idea
until the end
when we look back
and see the
uneaten banquet.*
—**Atticus**, *Love Her Wild*

I combed my fingers through my knotted, salty blonde hair as I drudged my legs out of the crashing waves of Huntington Beach's shore. As I looked down the coastline, thousands cheered as a ten-year-old boy named Matthew was submerged into the rough waters. One, two, three, four, five, six—it was hard to keep count of each person being baptized. "Is Jesus Christ your Lord and Savior?!" I screamed out into a $60 white megaphone.

"Could this actually be revival?" I whispered into my husband Parker's ear. It seemed as though God was moving in us and through us, like He said He would. Why now? Why us? Why summer 2020 in California?

The crowds thundered in praise and celebration for hours as people ran into the roaring waves to drown their sins and be born again. I cheered and splashed the water, but couldn't help feeling wildly distracted. In the corner of my eye, I could see the Huntington Beach police department sitting on the hoods of their black and white Ford trucks that were scattered across the bicycle path along the entrance to the beach near Lifeguard Tower 20. The sergeant sat on the hood of the truck, with his hands crossed over his knees, as I avoided eye contact to refrain from being arrested. I grabbed Parker and pulled him to the side, behind the lifeguard tower and asked, "How are you doing?"

In a low but steadfast tone, he responded, "I'm okay, this is just crazy," as he wrapped his fingers around a pale yellow citation for "illegal assembly."

A SIMPLE QUESTION
THAT WILL CHANGE YOUR LIFE

Only four years earlier, during winter 2016 while living in New York City, I had a conversation with God that changed *the entire trajectory of my life.*

My husband Parker and I had been praying for, believing for, and expecting a baby the entire year. I remember looking down at the pee-soaked stick in shock to see the little faint plus sign in the test window. Isn't it funny that when good things happen to us, we first expect them to not be real?

The first twelve weeks consisted of lots of migraines, throwing up, and constant nausea. Toward the end of my first trimester, Parker and I had both gotten the flu. The days were long as we rolled from one couch to the other, sipping Gatorade and slowly recovering.

It was after this whirlwind that God interrupted my life. It was an ordinary morning, before I had even gotten out of bed. I heard God ask me, *"Jessi, what do you look like fully alive?"*

The truth is, I didn't really know, nor had I stopped long enough to ask this question. I closed my eyes and whispered, "I don't know, Lord, please show me." To be honest, this wasn't an attempt for me to have a really radical, life-altering moment. In all actuality, I was being lazy and wanted my "quiet time" to include more sleep!

As I closed my eyes, I saw myself walking on a huge beach. I then saw a flash of different images. I smelled salty air and the scent of burning bonfires. Images of violent waves crashing on rocks, deep conversations about possibilities, dreams, and spiritual revelations. I saw strangers having God encounters saying, "Wow, Jesus is really real." There were flashes of me preaching with passion—on piers, under large circus tents, and at dining room tables. I saw myself cozy in an all-white hotel room, overlooking bluffs while writing and drinking tea out of a beautiful porcelain cup.

My soul immediately filled with hope.

The problem was, my life at the time didn't look anything like what I saw in this vision.

I knew something had to change.

So now, I ask you this same question.

What would your life look like if *you* were *fully alive?*

Hear me out.

I am not asking you what your life would look like if you were a better Christian or if you were finally recognized for all of your God-given talents and abilities. I am wanting you to take a moment, a breath, a "Selah" from the busyness of life and the constant distractions to ask the God of the universe what *you* look like when you are fully alive.

I know it seems like a funny question, but before we go on this journey of igniting revival together, we need to start by seeking Him.

I encourage you to take a moment, get alone with God, and ask Him what He has for *you*, here and now.

GOD IS GIVING YOU ACCESS

I have many tools, lessons, and avoidable "traps" that I want to share with you that *can* and *will* change your life. However, we first need a compass for the journey.

Where is true north? Where are we heading? Why?

Throughout this book, you will find little markers along your journey. The purpose of a trail marker (or *blaze*) is to help hikers follow a given path. This is where the word *trailblazer* comes from.

blaze \ 'blāz \
(noun)
1: an intensely burning fire
(transitive verb)
1: to mark (a trail) with blazes
2: to lead in some direction
Keep your eye out for the blaze!

YOUR FIRST BLAZE

I absolutely love the book of John. Out of all of the Gospels in the Bible, I could sit in John all day and discover something new over and over again.

Let's do a quick little dive into John 10. I promise you that the majority of this book is not a Bible study (although it probably should be and would do us all some good!), but I want to press into a vital "blaze" for our journey. In John 10, Jesus explains how one has access to the Kingdom of God through Him and Him alone. *There is no other way.* The Pharisees had put an immense amount of religious duty in between man and God. God is calling us, you and I, to not only enter into the Kingdom of God through our belief in Jesus Christ and His sacrifice, but He is giving us a significant *lesson into revival* that is often missed.

John 10:3-4 says:

> *And because the gatekeeper knows who he is, he opens the gate to let him in. And the sheep recognize the voice of the true Shepherd, for he calls his own by name and **leads them out,** for they belong to him. And when he has brought out all his sheep, he walks ahead of them and they will follow him, for they are familiar with his voice* (TPT).

Jesus is not only the Shepherd who allows us *in*— into unbroken fellowship with the Father—He is also the Shepherd who brings us *out!*

I believe that so often, as Christians, we are so excited that we get to enter *in* that we never access the *joy of going out.* However, Jesus is revealing to us a significant truth here. As we begin to press in, seek Him, and recognize His voice—we will be led out. It is *because* we belong to Him now that we are led out. Verse 4 then tells us the next clue. Once Jesus brings us out, He goes ahead of us and it's easy to follow Him because we *know* His voice.

Perhaps all of revival could be summed up in John 10. As we know Him, as we enter into the Kingdom of God through Jesus (and not our own works), He will lead us out, and we simply just need to follow as He leads.

Yet there is more.

I am freaking out because it gets so good!

Jesus then states in John 10:9, "I am the gate; whoever enters through me will be saved. They will come in and go out, and find pasture."

Alright, I am going to get all "theological" for five minutes. Here Jesus is saying, "I am the gate." The word *gate* in Greek is *thyra*. What this means is that Jesus is saying, "I am the portal, open door, the new opportunity." Everything is about to change. You now have access!

But access to what?

Access to salvation; or in Greek this word is *sozo*, meaning saved, healed, and delivered all in one.

Jesus is telling the religious leaders that the people now have an open door into the Kingdom. They can immediately be delivered out of danger, rescued from sin, be made well, and be healed in their body, soul, and spirit because of Him.

Now, here comes the million-dollar question.

John 10:10 is probably one of the most preached Scriptures and is one of my personal life verses. Jesus says, "The thief comes only to steal and kill and destroy; I have come that they may have life, and have it to the full."

So where have you been stolen from? What dreams have been killed? What doctor's report is destroying your hope? What news article is stealing your joy?

The word *destroy* also means "to cut off or to cancel." But I have good news.

You can't cancel Jesus.

Jesus is saying, "I have come, and where I am *there is life.*"

Not just a little bit of life. Not just a tiny bit of hope. Not just an experience at a conference where you continue to share the same story for the next 30 years.

He came so that you would have *life to the full.* A life that is greater, excessive, and more abundant than what you could imagine for yourself.

Saint Irenaeus once said, "The glory of God is man fully alive."

Are you fully alive today?

RECALIBRATE

So, before we continue on, let's pause for a moment and ask God what this "fully alive" life is like for *you.*

Read the following questions aloud and then close your eyes.

+ "Holy Spirit, what do I look like fully alive?"
+ "In what ways have I been stolen from that You want to restore?"
+ "What dreams have been destroyed that were from You?"

Then write down everything you see and hear.

What do you see?

What does the air smell like?

Who is around you?

Any other details, images, words, thoughts?

Ponder these things with the Lord and invite the Spirit to take you deeper.

This is where our journey begins.

CHAPTER 2

The End

Genuine revival begins when a person or a group of people have come to the end of their tether or rope. They have come to the end of their own transient resources and discovered the beginning of God's eternal, unlimited resources. This process is one of self-emptying, self-death even, in which we relinquish control to God and surrender ourselves to His love and power. When that happens the Holy Spirit comes, filling the empty spaces of our hearts.
—**Rolland Baker,** *Keeping the Fire*

In my early 20s, I had a purple candle with a quote etched into the side that sat on the windowsill of my small Manhattan apartment. My apartment was technically a one-bedroom that was converted into a two/three-bedroom by a temporary wall and a curtain in the living room. It smelled of kimchi from the culinary interests of my Korean roommate whom I found on a Craigslist ad. My mom had given me the candle for Valentine's Day when I was a senior in high school. Valentine's Day was always a special holiday in our home. As a child, we couldn't afford expensive outings, so my mom would prepare tomato soup from a can (because it was red) and make toast in the shape of a heart. We would sit on floor pillows and watch movies together while sipping on our hot soup.

Every year she would give me a box of truffles, and I would savor every bite. My favorite was the chocolate covered marzipan that melted in my hand, covering my dirty, half-painted pink fingernails. The Valentine's Day candle had an overly citrus smell that I didn't admire, but the quote about a caterpillar becoming a butterfly always resonated with me, which is why it made its way into my Manhattan apartment—a gentle reminder. One I very much needed on the evening that I contemplated ending my life.

The majority of my childhood I grew up with a single mom. At the mention of this, the first question people ask is, "Do you know your real dad?" I used to wrestle so much with this question. What exactly is a real dad? You see, I never met my biological father, and people are often confused by the fact that I have no intention to. I know that he was tan, attractive, and had blond hair based on one photograph that I have of him holding me as a baby. Call it blissful ignorance or whatever you'd like, but I prefer the imaginary version of this man. I sometimes pondered hiring a private investigator to locate my absent biological father, which led to terrifying thoughts of jail cells, egotistical stockbrokers, or possibly both.

The truth is, my mom did a great job raising me. The best job a 20-year-old single female with no real parents to call her own could do. I won't steal her story because she should write her own, but the facts of my mother's upbringing are gruesome to say the least. When I was nine years old, though, she met the most amazing man on planet earth, Tony. He legally adopted me when I was 11 years old and, to me, he is my real dad. Tony loved me really well. We had our special Starbucks dates, long conversations about music, and he helped me to get into college and prepare for the future. However, the thing I love the most about Tony is how much he loves my mom.

My mom, Ann, got introduced to Jesus while pregnant with me. As a young child, I'd sit on the kitchen counter and watch her fill those black marble composition journals with pages and pages of God encounters. The black writing was my mom's; the red writing was what Jesus was saying to her. She'd put Keith Green cassette tapes on in the living room, and blast "The Lord is my Shepherd, I shall not want" as loud as she could for all the neighbors to hear. She'd often recount how her pastor told her that she wasn't a loser, that God made her a winner. This may seem obvious to most Christians, but that was a refreshing revelation for a 20-something who was told she would never amount to anything by everyone around her.

My mom decided to be baptized in someone's backyard Jacuzzi while pregnant with me. I've always kind of joked that I was extra holy because I technically was baptized in my mother's womb.

A NEW YORK ROMANCE

I am one of those people who never sat and dreamed about living in Manhattan but more just ended up there. After graduating from University of Miami in Florida, I knew I had to leave Miami after cycles of bad relationships and toxic friendships. Once I moved to New York City, I very quickly started working for an entertainment company that ran private events and nightclubs in the bustling city. This was an attractive but low-paying job. It's weird to have an occupation that offers you status without the means to maintain it. I always felt like I was struggling. To be clear, living in Manhattan is often nothing like what you see in the movies. Running in Central Park is never followed by meeting an attractive Wall Street investor at the local coffee shop. The nights are long, and the city is cold. If you can afford to take a cab, there is a battle on the street to get it and you better be ready to fight.

One evening after working till 4 a.m., I ran three avenues in five-inch heels to catch a cab, only to have that dreamy Wall Street investor jump in before me and slam the door in my face. I wasn't a trust fund baby, and the glamorous life of the city always felt like one promotion away. On Thursday evenings, I would find myself rushing into Forever 21 to find a cheap dress to wear to a party after work. Later that evening, covered in face-paint and cranberry vodka, I would hunker down over my $75 bill for three Patron shots and sign "F you" in the tip area.

After being in Manhattan for six months, I started dating Drew. Drew was one of the characters you read about in a fiction novel; his personality was too big to be true. However, I will remind you this is a non-fiction story.

Drew was the kind of person that I would refer to as an LOP—"Life of the Party." When he arrived, everyone knew it and was happy he was there. He had nicknames for everything and funny ways of communicating that everyone attempted to copy with failed victory. For example, if Drew saw you in a bar and hadn't seen you in a while, he would say something like, "I haven't seen you since 'Nam.'" This referred to Vietnam. People cheerfully would laugh because of course Drew was not a veteran of the Vietnam War. If anyone else said this, it would sound stupid and possibly weird. That was never the case for Drew.

I remember the first time I ever went to Drew's apartment. As we walked in, the doorman gave him a low high five as they made a few quips about life. I remember thinking, *Wow, I have never seen a doorman so excited to see a tenant before.* I learned a magic trick from Drew that would forever change my career and life. *It's important to remember everyone's name because they matter.* Drew knew the waitress' name at the Mexican restaurant we would frequent, the Chinese man at the deli around the corner, the doorman of our favorite nightclub, and the billionaire CEO we would run into at our favorite steakhouse. He treated them all the same, and that mattered to people. My relationship with Drew escalated quickly. After one month of dating, we were living together and more in love than any couple I had ever met. While other couples argued over trivial things, Drew and I would watch the TV series *Lost* together on the couch, order expensive take-out, and drink champagne on the balcony of "our" apartment overlooking the Empire State building.

Drew's family was well known in my hometown and his family business name was plastered on nearly every street corner. I always felt compassion for Drew, for the pressure he was under to make a name for himself. Although I didn't grow up with two dimes to rub together, I at least had the freedom to discover my passions and purpose. Drew compensated for these pressures by proving to everyone that he had chosen this endeavor and was up for the challenge, while still enjoying a full life. Our adventures to foreign countries, experiencing exotic food, and laughing together as we crawled into our five-star hotel room washed away the long afternoons of touring offices, needing to say the right thing, and constantly presenting a "perfect" life.

I was Drew's safe place. We would drive through the city in his Range Rover on his way to his divorced mother's house as he would share with me fears and burdens no 22-year-old should wrestle with. I was the only one who knew the secret pain behind the flawless family portraits. Drew would drink more whiskey on the evenings that his mom would tell him about all of the alimony owed to her. We had both found "our person." Our relationship was a dream—but like all dreams, you always end up waking up abruptly.

TEAR SOAKED

When Drew and I ended our very serious relationship, it was as dramatic as any breakup should be. We had spent the evening at The Plaza Hotel and it was Valentine's Day. Now to clarify, The Plaza Hotel is a beautiful and nostalgic place to visit for any New Yorker. However, that wasn't the case here. Drew's dad had an apartment in The Plaza Hotel, and this was a last-ditch effort to salvage his lack of planning. I woke up frustrated that morning, facing the facts that the relationship had been struggling for the past month or so. After an argument in the lobby, Drew decided to leave and go get beers with a friend in town. I cried myself to sleep, face-planted in the most expensive pillows Manhattan had to offer.

The next morning, we took a quiet cab back to our apartment. This morning, there were no high fives given to anyone. As we entered the apartment, the sun shone brightly into our living room. The crust of mascara on my eyelids made it too hard to bear the burning light. I closed the blinds and sat in silence on the couch. To be honest, I don't really remember our fight. I threatened to leave, and he took the threat seriously, which is never what you intend when you make empty threats. As a naïve girl, you want someone to fight for you, and it is shocking when they don't. I should have known better. I decided it would be best to take a break and I would head to my parents' house on Long Island for the weekend.

I'll never forget packing my Louis Vuitton duffle in our bedroom, angrily thinking, *He will be so sorry for this*, as I stormed out of the apartment, slammed the metal door, and went down the elevator. As I hailed a cab on the corner, I noticed a broken red rose on the ground before my feet. I thought to myself, *How beautifully poetic*, and I trampled on its petals and covered my tear-soaked face with the hood of my sweatshirt. I was always a fan of poetry and secretly thought this would maybe be a beautiful part of our redemptive story.

About a month passed with little to no communication between Drew and me. We had a trip to L.A. planned, and I was so excited because I had never been to the West Coast. As the date for our trip approached without any calls from Drew, I realized that it may actually be over. Throughout my life, I was not inexperienced when it came to pain. As a child, I was sexually abused by my babysitter, diagnosed in high school with an "incurable" disease, saved myself for marriage only to be raped at 16—the list goes on, and I will probably write an entire book about how many times God has pulled me out of pain. However, I had never quite experienced grief in this way. It felt like, for once in my life, I had "paid my price" and was finally living the life that I so desperately strove for. Have you ever felt your heart burning inside of you so hot that you believe it would be less painful to extract it with your bare fingernails than have it continue to burn?

My friends gave me all of the advice that friends can give, but at some point you fulfill your quotient of how much you can talk about how sad you are. I started going out more and staying out later. I was hopeful that the burning would fade over time as long as I kept myself busy. Working full time made it exhausting to preserve an active social life driven by the need to never be alone. Cocaine was never an addiction for me but became a close friend that would help me stay out late and not be alone with the demons in my head.

UNLUCKY

St. Patrick's Day is a very strange holiday if you ask me. I am still not really sure why we celebrate it, but it's a guarantee that you will not be alone drinking. A few of my girlfriends and I decided to go to our favorite local bar on the Upper East Side. Dorrian's was famous for having a young, preppy, single crowd, and the manager had become a close friend. We danced and sang loudly at the back bar as I found bright green sunglasses to take a photo with. This is called a flirting accessory. I was a pro at finding items like this to bring more attention to myself, and it always worked like a charm. A crowd of tall, handsome lacrosse players surrounded me and offered to buy me shots. As the tallest one picked me up, I could see past his green collar the hint of the one person I was always secretly hoping to run into.

Drew approached with confidence, unwavering before the wall of testosterone that surrounded me. It honestly was annoying. I had imagined this exact situation so many times in my head and dreamed it would set him into a fit of rage. The fit never came. Drew said a silent hello and offered to buy me a drink. I quickly forgot about the shots waiting for me at the bar and conceded. We talked about nothing and shared meaningless exchanges. My friends watched from a distance while I clung to every word that he said. Then the words "I miss you" so silently left his lips that I almost missed it. In that very moment, I took a deep breath and exhaled. My last month of misery was over. I had served my time in emotional prison and we were going to work this out. Drew suggested we take a cab back to my place and discuss our relationship. We exited quickly and slipped into a cab that had a slight vanilla fragrance wafting in the air.

In my head I rehearsed how this discussion would go down. I would put on confidence like a shield and not allow him to realize the state of weakness that had become my present reality. I would allow him to apologize, and after some time I would gracefully forgive him. I would allow him to spend the night but would only agree to kiss him because we would need to take things slow and start all over again.

As we drove passed 42nd Street, Drew received a text. As I watched his face change, I knew that it wasn't good. Drew then said, "Hey Jess. I am going to have to drop you off. I have to go meet a client."

"But it's 2 a.m.? Who needs to see you at 2 a.m.?!" I asked.

"They are clients from out of town who are part of an important deal."

"Where are you meeting them? Can I just go?"

"Well, they are at a strip club and I am meeting them there."

That blistering heart that had been occupying my chest for the last month was now moving its way into my arms, legs, face, and fingers. I couldn't believe this was happening. This couldn't be happening.

"Are you serious right now?" I begged, hoping this was some kind of twisted joke.

There was no response.

As we turned down 31st Street to my apartment, the cab slowly came to a halt. The cab driver looked back in his rearview mirror, waiting to see how this nightmare would unfold. As I stepped out of the cab, Drew said, "I will call you tomorrow and we will talk, I promise."

I slammed the cab door and said, "I never want to speak to you again!" As my shaking fingers reached for my keys, I wondered why in the hell did I have so much stuff in my bag? The graffiti on my door was less wel-coming than a high-fiving doorman, but at this moment I was thankful no one was around.

I staggered up the stairs and entered my apartment that was the fur-thest thing from a home. I crawled into my bedroom and locked the door behind me. Fully clothed, I dragged myself into my squeaky full-size bed and roared into my pillow, screaming and demanding that the fire burning within me must be expelled. I never wanted to feel pain like this again. I never wanted to feel again. I hated Drew. I hated this apartment. I hated my life. I started to choke on the vomit rising up in my throat and tried to reach for pain medication that I had from my root canal that was absolutely expired. As I clamored around my apartment, gasping for breaths in between long groans, I tightly closed my eyes and screamed out, "If You are real, God, take this pain away!"

Immediately, peace filled my room.

All of Manhattan went silent outside my window.

I could not cry as I felt a warm river of love come over me. I lay still, in silence, as this powerful love was filling the deepest crevices of my heart. I could feel that God was in the room. Afraid to see Him, I put my head under the blanket and closed my eyes. I gently whispered, "If I can have a relationship with You, God, I will give up everything to know You."

THE END IS YOUR BEGINNING

Jesus called Peter to follow Him while he was still a fisherman. As he followed Jesus, Peter saw all kinds of miracles take place right in front of him. Then, as a part of his internship, Jesus sent him, along with the other disciples, to go preach the Kingdom of God and to display it publicly.

And when He had called His twelve disciples to Him, He gave them power over unclean spirits, to cast them out, and to heal all kinds of sickness and all kinds of disease (Matthew 10:1 NKJV).

As a new follower of Jesus, Peter was being sent out in power. Despite the areas in Peter's life that should have disqualified him, Peter was qualified because of an encounter with the living God on the shores of the sea. From this place, he developed a love for Jesus and slowly his faith increased. As Peter walked, one step at time, into his destiny, he learned to live a life of risk.

This internship cost Peter everything. I think that for many of us, as followers of Jesus, we haven't really counted the cost. Yeah, sure, we want the miracles, the blessing, the favor from on high. However, do we want Jesus enough that we would die for Him? That's a very different altar call than our typical "close your eyes, raise your hand, believe in Him, and ye shall be saved."

Jesus is calling you to come, now, on a journey of following Him. I mean, "get your hands dirty and lay down your life" kind of following. Revival simply won't come from some smooth prayers and Sunday church attendance. No. It can't come that way because Jesus is *worth* so much more. He is worth it all.

Before we move forward, we need to do another hard pause.

Is the Jesus you are following the real Jesus at all? Does He confront your sin, heal your pain, empower you to *go* and serve others in selfless love?

Jesus is so wildly uncomfortable, but I respect that. The Lion of Judah wants to be let out of the cage of what you believe a "good God" should be like. He has qualified you to transform nations. Why? Because He loves you. We *get* to serve God. We *get* to be a part of *His* mission here on earth. The privilege is overwhelming when you think about it. It's heartbreaking that even for a moment (or for some of us, years) we have allowed the enemy to rob us of such an incredible opportunity.

Jesus is saying to you right now, "Come. Come follow Me. I can take away your pain. I can give you a brand-new life. I can take your sin and exchange it for the Kingdom."

Do you believe Him?

Jesus answered him, "I assure you and most solemnly say to you, unless a person is born again [reborn from above—spiritually transformed, renewed, sanctified], he cannot [ever] see and experience the kingdom of God" (John 3:3 AMP).

CHAPTER 3

Jesus Is Really Real

Jesus did countless things that I haven't included here. And if every
one of his works were written down and described one by one, I
suppose that the world itself wouldn't have enough room to contain
the books that would have to be written!
—John 21:25 TPT

Often people say to me, "Jessi, I am not an evangelist. I am afraid to share the Gospel."

I simply just say to them, "Come, come and see. Once you encounter the living God and see His love for others, it is impossible to not talk about Him."

I truly believe that nothing robs us of God's promises more than the "religious spirit" and tiny deceptions we believe along the way. While we were still sinners, Christ died for us and paid the price for our sins. Afterward, He rose from the dead. We can hear this so much in church and easily neglect the power. Jesus really, actually died. This isn't a spiritual metaphor. He was dead-dead. Wrapped up in burial garments and in a tomb. You don't put someone in a tomb unless they are really, truly, absolutely dead.

Then, Jesus rose from the dead.

This is the central part of the Gospel, which many neglect to emphasize. We love that Jesus saved us from our sins, but He wasn't just a dead sacrifice; He is *alive!* Like, really, really alive! In John 14:18-21, Jesus on the way to the cross tells His disciples:

> I promise that **I will never leave you helpless** or abandon you as orphans—I will come back to you! Soon I will leave this world and they will see me no longer, but you will see me, because I will live again, **and you will come alive too**. So when that day comes, you will know that I am living in the Father and that you are one with me, for I will be living in you. Those who truly love me are those who obey my commands. **Whoever passionately loves me will be passionately loved by my Father. And I will passionately love you in return and will manifest my life within you** (TPT).

Jesus is actually alive and wants to have a relationship with us. I sang about it for years in church but still never "got it." I now hold these verses like a treasure. The fact that Jesus rose from the dead means that these words are true. He will never leave you because He is not dead, but alive! I don't know about you, but for me that changes everything. That means that I can hear from God, I can know what He is doing on the earth, I can feel His love for me and for others. It means that when I pray, He is actually listening. He says, "Those who truly love Me are those who obey My commands." This isn't about obeying commands to earn His love! He is telling us that "When you really know Me, when you have experienced My love for you, you will obey Me." If you have a hard time obeying God, pay attention to this next part!

THE SCRIPTURES ARE ABOUT...

When talking to the Pharisees, Jesus said:

> *You have your heads in your Bibles constantly because you think you'll find eternal life there. But you miss the forest for the trees. These Scriptures are all about me! And here I am, standing right before you, and you aren't willing to receive from me the life you say you want* (John 5:39-40 MSG).

The Pharisees were the people who knew Scripture better than anyone. They were so stuck in pondering the laws of Moses that they missed the presence of God. My heart aches when I read these words. I believe Jesus is speaking to each one of us *now*. We want some other way; we want some magic method. We want supernatural lives, but we don't want *Him!*

Jesus goes on to say:

> *I do not accept glory from human beings, but I know you. I know that you do not have the love of God in your hearts. I have come in my Father's name, and you do not accept me; but if someone else comes in his own name, you will accept him. How can you believe since you accept glory from one another but do not seek the glory that comes from the only God?* (John 5:41-44)

OOF!
Selah.

How did Jesus know that they didn't have the love of God in their hearts? Jesus came in His Father's name, which means that He came in the Father's authority, not His own. Jesus leads the way in humility and confronts those with pride. When we read the Scriptures, we should leave more humble, more in awe of how big God is, and thankful for His love for us. If our Bible studies, evangelism campaigns, Facebook ministries, or book deals lead to an inflated ego and not a humble, repentant heart, then we must lay it all down and do so quickly. I find that Jesus reveals more of who He is to those with pure motives, whose hearts burn to know Him above all things.

HE MAY NOT BE THE MESSIAH YOU WANT; HE IS THE MESSIAH YOU NEED

As I have been praying recently, I keep hearing that "the lion wants out of the cage." Jesus never pulls punches to please the crowd. He didn't use the Scriptures to flatter His hearers or to make them think that God was pleased with them if He was not. When you read Scripture, when you spend time in His presence, there should be times when you feel challenged. Jesus is so often not the kind of Messiah we think we want. One scroll on social media, and we can see so many ministry leaders playing the same cards that the Jews did when Christ came to earth. Yes, of course, we mock the Pharisees in our preaching, but don't we do the same thing?

They wanted a political messiah who could deliver them from Rome and provide peace and prosperity. How much has changed? If He had satisfied their tastes, Jesus could have been a popular leader and a rich megachurch pastor. After He fed the multitudes, He knew that they wanted to come and take Him by force to make Him king. Jesus just doesn't do things the way we would. Jesus withdrew to the mountain by Himself, all alone (see John 6:15). I wonder how many of us, myself included, need to continue to learn these lessons from Him? Jesus refused the popular way for the way of the Father. Jesus would not falsely convey who He is to gain a following.

Savage Jesus warned the Pharisees that their rejection of Him made them susceptible to follow false messiahs who came in their own name. Later on, as Jesus spoke about the end times, He warned of false prophets who will arise and lead many astray. Accompanying this deception, people's love for God will grow cold (see Matt. 24:11-12).

I believe that for so many of us, our Christianity isn't working because we want a more comfortable Jesus. We are prone to follow false teachers because it "feels good." Paul the apostle later warned:

> *For the time will come when they will not endure sound doctrine; but wanting to have their ears tickled, they will accumulate for themselves teachers in accordance to their own desires, and will turn away their ears from the truth and will turn aside to myths* (2 Timothy 4:3-4 NASB).

We see the same thing today—focus on the positive, never confront sin, and you'll have a large congregation or a large social media following.

IS IT WORKING?

Many of you have heard about Jesus, but you may feel like you don't *really* know Him. You may identify as a Christian, but it seems like other people have some kind of magical special access. If your Christianity is not "working," it may be a good idea to take a pause and find out why.

When we first moved to California, we had a used 2010 Jeep Commander. At one point, the engine light kept turning on when we'd start the car in colder weather. It would never light in warm Orange County, but on cold road trips, there would go that good ol' engine light. Do you know what we did? We ignored it.

Of course not. We took the car in to a mechanic to check what was wrong. It turned out that it was nothing major, we simply needed to get a new battery. When we have problems with our cars, we know to take them in to get fixed. Yet our faith could be completely failing and we don't stop, pause, and think, *Hey, maybe something is wrong here. Maybe I need to fix something.*

I think for many of us, we can end up adhering to a culture of Christianity in which Christ is not involved at all.

I know this seems incredibly harsh, but it's a reality that is wildly impacting the nations. I don't want you to continue reading this book, learn some new tools, launch some big evangelism campaign, and still not know Christ intimately.

If you want revival, you must truly and deeply *know* the Reviver.

I know, it almost seems too simple.

Turning around, Jesus saw them following and asked, "What do you want?"

They said, "Rabbi" (which means "Teacher"), "where are you staying?"

*"Come," he replied, "**and you will see**."*

So, they went and saw where he was staying, and they spent the day with him (John 1:38-39).

To give you a little bit of context here, Jesus had just started His public ministry. He was demonstrating the Kingdom of God that is now available to everyone, and He was inviting these onlookers to come and follow Him into this new life. I find it interesting that the early disciples said to Him, "Where are You staying?" It's kind of a strange question. He replies by saying to them, "Come, and you will see." Jesus starts off His ministry by offering an invitation. He says to them, "Come."

COME AND SEE

The way that He gathered His very first disciples was a simple invitation to "come and see." The Greek word for *see* is the word *horaó*, which actually means, "behold, perceive, see" or properly, "to stare at, to discern clearly (physically or mentally); by extension, to attend to; to experience" (Strong's, G3708).

Jesus is actually saying to His first followers, "Come and experience everything I am talking about. Come behold, discern, perceive, and attend to the Kingdom life." He's not merely trying to teach them something. He's trying to give them an entirely different experience of *living*.

Then later, in John 1:46, we see Jesus gather more disciples and have an encounter with Phillip. Guess what happens to Phillip after his encounter? He *goes* to find his friend Nathaniel and tells him, "We have found the one Moses wrote about in the Law, and about whom the prophets also wrote—Jesus of Nazareth, the son of Joseph." Nathaniel responds, "Can anything good come out of Nazareth?"

Isn't this this world we live in? We expect God to move in a certain way, through certain people, in certain places that we call "holy" like our church buildings. Yet He is so much more creative than that. For years, people have prophesied death and destruction over California saying, "Can anything good come out of California?" Yet here we are! Seeing revival being birthed once again in the place the religious have turned their backs on. Philip said to Nathaniel, "Come and see." He urged his friend to come and experience this Kingdom life that they had been searching for. Phillip gives us a "blaze" on our journey to encountering a *real Jesus*. He doesn't tell Nathaniel what he thinks he knows; *he offers him an invitation to come and see for himself.*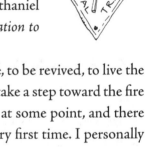

So here we are. If you are ready to come alive, to be revived, to live the life you were created for, I want to invite you to take a step toward the fire of His presence. Many of you have prayed this at some point, and there are some of you who are praying this for the very first time. I personally regularly pray this prayer as a reminder of the decision I have made to follow Jesus.

Pray this out loud with me:

Jesus,

I believe in You. You are real, Lord!

Thank You for forgiving me of my sins when You died on the cross.

Thank You for Your sacrifice for me to live free from sin and shame.

Forgive me, Lord.

Jesus, I believe in You. I believe You died and rose again.

Fill me with Your Holy Spirit.

Heal my heart, heal my mind, fill with me the same power that raised You from the dead! Empower me to live for You, and not for myself, every day of my life.

CHAPTER 4

Are You a Watcher
or a Fire Starter?

Be fearless in the pursuit of what sets your soul on fire.
—Jennifer Lee

When all of the wildfires started to spread throughout California, I started to study wildfires. I wanted to see if I could find a prophetic clue to what the Lord was doing in California specifically. I believe that often there is a connection between the natural and the supernatural. I learned quickly that with wildfires, they burn up what is dead. When the fires spread and the dead is cleared, it actually releases seeds into the ground that could never have been released without the fire. The fire clears every thistle, weed, and decay to make space for a new foundation of growth—and, most importantly, new life. This can be either encouraging or incredibly disheartening depending on what you are made of in the fire.

I believe that God is a consuming fire and that His Spirit burns rampant. Jesus wants *all* of us, every part. He wants a Church (big "C" Church) that is full of power and not "playing Christianity." The Word of God says in Matthew 11:12 that the Kingdom suffers violence and the violent take it by force. There is no room for sitting back and living an apathetic life in the Kingdom.

CALIFORNIA IS BURNING

The last few years, watching the fires grow in size in California, I can't help but wonder if this is the *kairos* moment to bring hope and share the Gospel. *Kairos* is one of the Greek words in the New Testament for "time." It is translated as "the right time," "a set or proper time, opportunity, due season, short time," or "a fixed and definite time, the time when things are brought to crisis, the decisive epoch waited for" (Strong's, G2540).

I believe God is giving us a prophetic word for this moment out of Hebrews 12:26-29:

> *At that time his voice shook the earth, but now he has promised, Once more I will shake not only the earth but also the heavens."* The words "once more" **indicate the removing of what can be shaken**—*that is, created things—so that what cannot be shaken may remain. Therefore, since we are receiving a kingdom that cannot be shaken, let us be thankful, and so worship God acceptably with reverence and awe, for our* **"God is a consuming fire."**

In the midst of so much loss, distress, shaking, and confusion spreading across this state that I now call home, I was stirred with conviction, wondering what God was wanting us to do in response.

Isaiah 33:14-15 says, "'Who of us can dwell with the consuming fire? Who of us can dwell with everlasting burning?' Those who walk righteously and speak what is right."

The Father despises lukewarm Christianity that just morphs into culture, is obsessed with fitting in, and is essentially "non-essential." I believe through the kindness and mercy of God, He has allowed 2020 to shake what can be shaken so that we, His Bride, can see what we're working with. The fire of God is consuming what is dead and exposing the brambles. I think what is the most shocking in this season is how much overgrowth we have allowed to consume what is meant to be holy and pure. It's amazing, though, that through His consuming fire He's giving us new seeds for renewal, which He is unleashing *His* way.

Are you hungering for the real thing? Do you feel like there has to be more to Christianity than what you're experiencing? Is your Christianity really working?

God is releasing a fresh fire, new seeds, and fertile soil for you to experience exponential acceleration in your pursuit of Him and His Kingdom. Don't give up now; it is just the beginning! You may be a part of the remnant seed that God is releasing on the earth. God is looking for a people who are not just wanting to pursue comfort or live by the status quo, but who are willing to go all in with what He is doing.

WHAT IS REVIVAL?

How does revival start? Why do revivals start in some places and not others? Why do some people get to be a part of revival while others do not? These are all questions I have personally wrestled with and have been asked over email and messages so many times.

Charles G. Finney is one of my favorite revivalists. He led the Second Great Awakening, and historians believe that he had one of the greatest spiritual impacts on modern-day Christianity and evangelism. He is known as the "Father of Modern Revivalism." So, for a moment, let's forget all of our opinions on revival and see what Father Finney tells us revival is.

What A Revival Is [Yeah, Finney is that blunt!]

It presupposes that the Church is sunk down in a backslidden state, and a revival consists in the return of the Church from her backslidings, and in the conversion of sinners.

1. A revival always includes conviction of sin on the part of the Church. Backslidden professors cannot wake up and begin right away in the service of God, without deep searchings of heart. The fountains of sin need to be broken up. In a true revival, Christians are always brought under such conviction; they see their sins in such a light that often they find it impossible to maintain a hope of their acceptance with God. It does not always go to that extent, but there are always, in a genuine revival, deep convictions of sin, and often cases of abandoning all hope.

2. Backslidden Christians will be brought to repentance. A revival is nothing else than a new beginning of obedience to God. Just as in the case of a converted sinner, the first step is a deep repentance, a breaking down of heart, a getting down into the dust before God, with deep humility, and a forsaking of sin.

3. Christians will have their faith renewed. While they are in their backslidden state they are blind to the state of

sinners. Their hearts are hard as marble. The truths of the Bible appear like a dream. They admit it to be all true; their conscience and their judgment assent to it; but their faith does not see it standing out in bold relief, in all the burning realities of eternity. But when they enter into a revival, they no longer see "men as trees, walking," but they see things in that strong light which will renew the love of God in their hearts. This will lead them to labor zealously to bring others to Him. They will feel grieved that others do not love God, when they love Him so much. And they will set themselves feelingly to persuade their neighbors to give Him their hearts. So their love to men will be renewed. They will be filled with a tender and burning love for souls. They will have a longing desire for the salvation of the whole world. They will be in an agony for individuals whom they want to have saved their friends, relations, enemies. They will not only be urging them to give their hearts to God, but they will carry them to God in the arms of faith, and with strong crying and tears beseech God to have mercy on them, and save their souls from endless burnings.

4. A revival breaks the power of the world and of sin over Christians. It brings them to such vantage ground that they get a fresh impulse towards heaven; they have a new foretaste of heaven, and new desires after union with God; thus the charm of the world is broken, and the power of sin overcome.

5. When the Churches are thus awakened and reformed, the reformation and salvation of sinners will follow. Their hearts will be broken down and changed. Very often the most abandoned profligates are among the subjects. Harlots, and

drunkards, and infidels, and all sorts of abandoned characters, are awakened and converted. The worst of human beings are softened and reclaimed, and made to appear as lovely specimens of the beauty of holiness.[1]

From one who pioneered revivalism and stewarded it well during his lifetime, there is a lot we can learn from Finney to apply to modern day.

"CHRISTIANITY IS NOT A SPECTATOR SPORT"

Billy Graham once said, "Christianity is not a spectator sport. It's something in which we become totally involved."

If you ask a majority of Christians today, "Is Christianity working for you?" their response would be "no" or "kind of."

Personally, I have become a Christian four times. I grew up in the Vineyard church and attended the Toronto Blessing at seven years old. When I was nine, we moved and attended a church that taught Scripture but never taught about the Holy Spirit or how to have a relationship with Jesus. As a teenager, I began to believe that the "Christian life" was for the boring, so I went after an extravagant life that the world offered me—luxury Manhattan apartment, access to VIP rooms in the city's most exclusive nightclubs, working hard, hustling harder. This only led to cocaine binges, depression, multiple abortions, anxiety, and suicidal thoughts. Then, on that cold random night, I found the living God. I began a journey of a life full of miracles, healing, God's extreme love, and supernatural encounters.

In 2016, my husband Parker and I moved across the country from New York City to California to be a part of the revival God showed us during a month of fasting and prayer.

We quit our jobs in ministry, sold most of our belongings, and moved across the country in our Jeep Commander. We based this move on several visions and revelations that had come in relation to preaching the Gospel, making disciples, and igniting revival. We believed then, and still do today, that God is stirring a revival in California that will ignite the nation. *We are **all in** on that belief and promise.*

The things that you believe should cost you something. Conviction doesn't have a small price tag. It's expensive. I'm talking Gucci expensive.

When we first arrived in California, we shared the Gospel through street evangelism methods, treasure hunts, and door-to-door ministry. (That was really awkward!) We launched our first micro church and called it "Salt." Old wineskins are hard to shed, so we made a pretty Instagram profile and launched an "intro barbecue" to share the vision and values of our "new" idea for a disciple-making church. At our first barbecue, we had about 60 people show up. We were very excited! Then Parker shared what would later be the kiss of death to our "big launch."

He said, "We are going to make disciples. Everyone in this church will be expected to share the Gospel and make disciples. If you belong to another church (or several churches), we encourage you to not church shop, and go back to your church and serve there. This won't be the right church for you."

I cringed.

I knew that the little momentum we had to launch our church was killed. Up until this point, all of our "church planting training" primarily depended on good marketing, a *big* launch, and transfer growth from other churches. Parker wanted to flip the model on its head and actually plant churches with new believers. Silence filled the room. The next week, about eight people showed up in our tiny apartment living room. Parker taught from Scripture, we worshiped with music playing from our television, and he taught them how to make disciples who multiply through evangelism and "unbroken fellowship" with Jesus.

It was a slow, humbling, and brutal process. I think I cried once a week. If I am honest, I hated this church we were being called to lead. I hated having to explain to all of our friends in ministry what we were doing. I couldn't stand having another conversation with the weird person who showed up at our front door all bitter and offended by their last church.

We live in such an interesting time as a Christian culture. Those who are forerunning and pioneering new things are often viewed as rebels to the establishment. I've heard a handful of sermons about how innovative God is, how He is the Creator of all things, yet we so rarely innovate with Him. So many people have asked us, "Are micro churches the 'new' way that church will be done?" Our flesh is desperate to create a system to the ways of God. However, Jesus is just wilder than that. As soon as you have Him figured out, He's off cleansing lepers, having dinner with prostitutes, and telling the crowd to eat His flesh. I firmly believe that God longs to innovate with us. He deeply desires intimacy, and I think He has so many incredibly creative solutions for us if we would simply lay down our systems and seek Him.

Prophetic note in my journal from Parker, May 2013

Lighthouse - light covers Atlanta, reaches back to
- Baptisms in the ocean
- Multitudes
- Tent full of light
- Sunrise
- Rumors of the good news
- Wind / Water flood
- War by night
- More with us than with them
- Ring of light surrounding the city
- Key with two parts Jesus held, open the door to city if we both held it
- Flaming arrow across long island

(Parker - 1/2013)

IN YOUR HANDS

Smith Wigglesworth was a powerful evangelist who led revival in the late 1800s. He worked as a plumber and became so transformed by the power of God that he had to lay down his trade to continue his ministry of preaching in power, raising the dead, and healing the sick. I personally love reading about Smith Wigglesworth because he shows us an important "blaze" to revival—*once an ordinary man recognizes that Jesus is truly alive, he is empowered through the Holy Spirit to do extraordinary things.* If you are reading this book, I can imagine that you are like me in your desire to be used by God.

Smith Wigglesworth once wrote:

> When the Spirit of the Lord is upon us we impart not words, *but life.* Words are only that you may understand what the Word is, but the Word is really life-giving. *So when we are covered with the Spirit we are imparting life.* ...If you are ready to receive it, it is amazing how it will quicken your mortal body every time you touch this life. It is divine life. It is the life of the Son of God.[2]

The reality is many Christians don't understand that Jesus has already won. He is the Victor over death, sin, and every battle against the enemy. As believers, we are going into a battle reminding the enemy that he has already been defeated. Jesus is saying, "Go." He is saying that He's given us authority. Yes, revival comes from God, but don't believe for a minute that you don't have a part to play. Awakening will be stirred across our nations when believers begin to believe. This isn't someone else's responsibility. Those days of waiting for the big evangelist to come into town are changing. You and I, together, we need to repent from our sins and return to the foundations of our faith.

I am still amazed that people could be in a church for a year and have never shared the Gospel once. As leaders, are we focused on making "good church members" and not equipping people for real life as ministers of the Gospel?

IG·NI·TION
I.NISH(ə)N
NOUN.
THE ACTION OF SETTING SOMETHING ON
FIRE OR STARTING TO BURN.

FIRE STARTER

Matthew 3:11 says, "He will baptize you with the Holy Spirit and fire."

We have not been given the Holy Spirit for simply an ecstatic experience. We have not been ignited in His fire to simply sit contained, quiet, and without purpose. While I love having encounters with God, getting a prophetic word, uncontrollable laughter, and more, God has given us the Holy Spirit so that we may be witnesses. Witnesses of His good news! That we would be bold in saying, "This is the Jesus I know. This is the Gospel! I was separated from God because of sin, but God loves me so much that He sent His Son Jesus down to earth to die on the cross as a sacrifice for my sin. Even if you don't believe in Jesus, He died for you. Best of all, He rose again! That means that you can live a brand-new life."

Evangelist Reinhard Bonnke once wrote:

> The church of Christ is a "go" church, not a "sit" church. Look outward, to where our Lord is moving across the continents. Some are looking inward, everlastingly examining their own souls, incapacitated by introspection. Jesus is saving you— fear not. Now start helping Him to save others.[3]

As my husband and I have recently stepped into leading revival across the beaches of California and in tents on open fields, I am stirred to believe that this moment in history is an invitation for *every believer*. I am praying and hoping that my words challenge the false promises of religion, culture, and patchy new age philosophy. Through these messy, blunt, transparent pages, I invite you into a Christian life that you may have never been told is real or possible.

What would you do if nothing was impossible? If you were living fully alive and full of vision for your city and nation? What if fear of man, depression, shame, and the many things that keep us silent were no longer an issue?

Imagine a world ignited with the fiery love of Jesus and the power of the Holy Spirit. Imagine an unstoppable Church that let go of the status quo and became more concerned about preaching the Gospel than filling up a building. Could this be the very moment in history when we yield our ways and partner with God for a harvest of souls that ushers in the return of Jesus?

Will you join me in revolting against apathy and ignite the world around you with God's love and power? Together, we can be a part of something bigger than ourselves. If you are holding this book in your hands, it is not a coincidence.

You are a part of the remnant army that is rising.

NOTE

1. Charles Finney, "What a Revival of Religion Is," (Public Domain, 1835), Teaching American History, https://teachingamericanhistory.org/library/document/what-a-revival-of-religion-is.

2. Smith Wigglesworth, *Manifesting the Power of God* (Shippensburg, PA: Destiny Image Publishers, 2016), 11.

3. Reinhard Bonnke, *Evangelism by Fire* (Lake Mary, FL: Charisma House, 2011), 21.

PART 2

Rites of Passage

*Suppose that God has **especially promised** the thing. ...We are bound to believe that we shall receive it when we pray for it. You have no right to put in an **if**, and say, "Lord, **if it be thy will**, give us thy Holy Spirit." This is to insult God. To put an **if** into God's promise, where God has put none, is tantamount to charging God with being insincere.*

—Charles Finney,
Lectures on Revival of Religion, *"The Prayer of Faith"*

CHAPTER 5

Golden Journey

There will come a time, you'll see, with no more tears.
And love will not break your heart, but dismiss your fears.
Get over your hill and see what you find there,
With grace in your heart and flowers in your hair.
—Mumford and Sons, "After the Storm"

I recently came across this beautiful artwork called kintsugi. I was brought to tears because I couldn't believe such a beautiful thing existed.

Kintsugi is a Japanese art of repairing broken pottery by mending the areas of breakage with lacquer dusted or mixed with powdered gold, silver, or platinum, a method similar to the maki-e technique. As a philosophy, it treats breakage and repair as part of the history of an object, rather than something to disguise.[1]

These amazing masters of the art do years of training and they take broken pottery, what others would call "garbage," and they fill it with gold. Kintsugi is also called the "golden joinery."

When the artist takes the time to put the gold in every broken layer, all of a sudden what was deemed "garbage" has increased in value because of the artist's touch. Sometimes, it takes several months to put one of these delicate pots back together because of the labor that goes into putting the gold neatly into every crevice and making sure that it's absolutely restored.

This is what our God does.

He takes every broken part of our lives, every mistake, every moment that we regret, and He says, "I love you, I can restore you. And guess what? I'm actually going to use those wounds to bring healing, if you will trust Me." Then, He fills us with gold and all we have to do is yield to the Artist. We simply say, "I'll surrender. I'll let You put gold in that hidden space." The greatest moment in life is when the Artist trains us to do the same thing for others. He takes His time to teach us the art of restoring and filling others' broken pieces with gold as well.

LIFE RESTORED

There's a story in the Bible in which Jesus restored a woman who was broken. This woman sticks out to me because in the midst of the crowd, Jesus noticed her. I feel so challenged because sometimes it's so hard to just stop and see someone. I believe that God can give us the ability to see like He sees and start to love others lavishly.

In this account, Jesus was on His way to minister somewhere else when He encountered a law breaker, a woman who had been bleeding for twelve years. According to Mosaic law, she was unclean. She should not have even been in that crowd. Society had already discarded her, thrown her away. The law said that she could not come near anyone, that she was dirty and an outcast of society.

While Jesus was on His way, the woman saw Him and in desperation grabbed on to His robe. She knew that just a touch could change everything for her. She reached out and grabbed the hem of His robe. In that moment, she experienced the glory of Heaven on earth. She had an encounter with God on an ordinary day in an ordinary place.

What I believe is one of the most amazing statements in the New Testament happened right after that moment. In Matthew 9:22, it says Jesus *turned.*

> But Jesus turning and seeing her said, "Take courage, daughter; your [personal trust and confident] faith [in Me] has made you well." And at once the woman was [completely] healed (AMP).

Jesus turned. He turned and He stopped and He saw her. She was probably expecting Jesus to be upset with her because the law told her that she could not touch or be around anyone, that she was broken, that she was discarded.

Jesus is turning toward you, now, if you would simply reach out to Him. This little act of faith, of reaching out to touch Him, will change everything for you.

BURNED OUT

When we first moved to California, I kept meditating on this verse in Matthew 11:28-30 that says:

> *Are you tired? Worn out? Burned out on religion? Come to me. Get away with me and you'll recover your life. I'll show you how to take a real rest. Walk with me and work with me—watch how I do it. Learn the unforced rhythms of grace. I won't lay anything heavy or ill-fitting on you. Keep company with me and you'll learn to live freely and lightly* (MSG).

Gosh, I was so tired. I felt so confused. I felt like God had abandoned me, as if He had forgotten every prophetic word and promise over my life. A month after moving across the country in 2016, I had gotten pregnant again! I had a three-month-old baby and was going to give birth to another baby in only nine months! We had no friends or family in California. Everyone we knew and loved were settled in New York, Washington, and Australia. At this point, no one cared about micro churches or what we were doing. All speaking engagements stopped. Our salary and health insurance ended, and financially we were at the end of our savings.

Parker picked up a few personal training clients at Equinox gym. He would wake up at 5 a.m. to train, then come home around noon to take care of our son David while I worked on a few freelance social media campaigns for luxury brands. Throughout the night, I would wake up to nurse our baby while sending out emails to potential social media clients because we could barely make rent for our small apartment, all while being pregnant.

Was this what God had us leave everything for?

One evening, we went to the outdoor mall with the three people we were discipling—Joe Ferguson, Taylor Hill (now Ferguson), and Victoria Castillo. We went on a treasure hunt to prophesy, share the Gospel, and see the supernatural in Huntington Beach. After a few hours out, we saw no divine encounters, no miracles, and no salvations. I was embarrassed and felt like I had nothing to offer anyone.

The next day, Parker and I put our baby David in the stroller and walked down Huntington Beach's bike path toward the pier. I sat on a rock wall and just fell apart. I put my hands over my face and wept, and just kept on weeping.

"Parker, I can't do this anymore. Where is God? Did we hear Him wrong? Did we make a huge mistake? I hate this. I feel like a fraud. We are teaching about the power of God but there is no power. Nothing is working. I don't even know who I am anymore. It feels like we took a hundred steps backward from our calling!"

Parker sat silently looking out at the horizon.

I wanted to kill him. I felt my fingers begin to clench and rage rise up my neck. How could he just sit there in silence while I'm hysterically crying?

He then looked at me and said, "I know. I feel frustrated too."

That was it!

No plan, no encouragement that things were going to change, no "word" from the Lord!

That evening we had a micro church gathering in our home. About eight people joined us and sat on our carpeted apartment floor. I cried and said to the group, "I have nothing to share. I want to see the power of God and I'm not seeing it. I have nothing to teach you."

Parker stood up and said, "We are going to play worship music on the TV. Let's just worship Him."

The first 30 minutes were so incredibly awkward. I sat on the couch with my face in my sweaty palms, my mind was spinning. My soul was tattered cloth. My spirit was like a wilted daisy. It felt as if everything I had believed about God had come to an end, all the romanticism was gone, and I refused to continue with the religious charades. I did not want to worship God.

Some of the girls in the group moved to the floor, open handed, and sang alongside the TV. Parker paced back and forth in the kitchen as Joe stood by the doorway, singing as loud as he could as his veins popped out of his neck with each chorus.

After several hours, something happened.

God met us right there, on that cream-colored carpet. Just a handful of millennials, worshiping, pleading with God, refusing to "fake" their Christianity for another moment. The presence of God swept into the room. I opened my eyes and could notice that everyone felt something shift. I didn't know what was happening, but I felt a glimmer of hope rise.

GOOD NEWS SPREADS

So many of us want our churches to look like the early Church, but we find in Scripture that the early disciples never stopped teaching and proclaiming the Good News. I'll repeat that—they *never stopped*. In Acts 5:42, it says, "Day after day, in the temple courts and from house to house, they *never stopped* teaching and proclaiming the good news that Jesus is the Messiah." They went from house to house; they went into every public arena. They went to the temple courts, which is where the religious people were, which shows me that sometimes you can lead someone who seems "religious" to Christ.

I believe that there is something that happens in our faith journey when we decide to just "never stop." I mean, when you become so resolute in your belief in the power of Jesus that no criticism, disappointment, pandemic, or preference can stop you from proclaiming the Good News. Could this next revival be led by the most unknown Jesus followers who have just made a decision to keep proclaiming the Gospel, unglamorously, just disciplined and calendarized every week, or even every day?

Are you waiting for God to give you something better than Jesus and the power of the Holy Spirit? Perhaps the thing that America is searching for has already come. If only the Church could be convinced. The good news is that Jesus is in charge—He has all authority. Perhaps our identities and callings become so burdensome when we are trying to orchestrate them outside of Christ.

So the question really is, why don't we share the Gospel? Maybe some of us haven't been convinced that Jesus really is all that we want. When we moved here, I thought, *Yeah, I am all in.* Till the testing came. Till everything that my identity had been built on was stripped away. Till it was Jesus plus nothing and He was all I had.

I am so thankful that I grew up in a Christian home; that my mom brought me to church, played worship music in the house, and hosted Bible studies. Although I wasn't fully following Jesus, I grew up hearing the Good News that was available to me. In my darkest hour, the seed that my mom had deposited was sprouting. When everything fell apart, my soul knew what my mind did not. My spirit cried out to God to rescue me, although my flesh was revolting in rebellion against Him.

However, so many people in this world don't have the opportunity to grow up in Christian homes and have those foundations and seeds of faith invested into them. Scripture says in Romans 10:14, "How can they hear without someone preaching to them?" Perhaps, just maybe, that someone is you. Perhaps it's me. Maybe, just maybe, it's everyone who actually calls themselves a Christian.

SPIRITUAL GIFTS

The first woman I ever led to the Lord (intentionally) was in Byron Bay during a year-long mission trip called The World Race in 2010. After an afternoon of being trained in street evangelism by my friend Daniel, I was apathetic toward the "outreach" scheduled that afternoon. I wanted to do something that felt more "organic." The thought of approaching a stranger and offering to pray for them felt awkward, weird, and embarrassing. I initially hated it and I had the biggest attitude in the group. We hosted a 24-hour prayer at the beach and offered to pray for anyone who came by. Down the road, I saw a woman who seemed lonely. I decided to leave the group and walk over. She reeked of cheap vodka and her eyes stared down at me. I could feel her brokenness. I saw myself in her. In clubs in New York City—I, too, had been alone, reeking of vodka without any sense of hope or life.

I asked her if I could pray for her. We sat and talked for over an hour, and I prayed healing over her mind. She told me it was the first time she could feel God's love for her. I felt it too. She said she wanted to follow Jesus. I was in shock. Someone I had talked to actually wanted to follow Jesus!

Later that night, I was going into the bars in Byron to encourage and prophesy over girls in the bathrooms. I walked out of the bar and saw the woman from earlier that day on the corner crying. She shared with me that she had nowhere to go. A few of my friends and I walked with her down the street, away from the bars, and found a safe place for her to rest. She asked me to sing over her to help her sleep. My insecurities rose up because I'm not a good singer. I decided to abandon my discomfort in exchange for her comfort. I sang the only Christian song I knew, one my mother sang to me as a little girl, "Thy Word is a lamp unto my feet and a light unto my path." We cried together as she fell asleep in my arms.

After that, I was an evangelist.

Yet now, ten years later, I had a "spiritual gift" identity crisis. We are seeing revival spring forth and a million prophetic words come into fruition, and I feel like everything I have known about myself is being questioned and tested. As revival begins, I find ministry offices (such as apostle, teacher, prophet, pastor, evangelist) flying around like a pigeon trapped in a small bedroom.

"This person is more of a prophet and needs to decide this."

"We need to invite this person to speak at this event because they are an apostle and that's what this area needs."

"You have no role; your job is to make room for everyone else's gift-ings."

I received so many emails and messages about the calling on "our lives," and I couldn't hear God above the noise. I sat on the couch and looked up at Parker and said, "Babe, maybe I am not an evangelist. Maybe I am a prophet? How do I know what my spiritual gift is? What should my role in Saturate be? How do I lead all of these people who are more gifted than I am?"

Parker gave me the response that I didn't want.

He said, "Don't worry about what your gift is. Keep your focus on Jesus and just see what you do as you follow Him."

The best spiritual gifts test you can take is your life.

At the end of the day, you can take every personality and spiritual gifts assessment and still be left in confusion. There are so many self-proclaimed "whatevers," but at the end of the day, this is about what you *actually* do when you follow Him. What areas of your life has God redeemed for you to bring redemption to others? When you spend time with Jesus and follow Him, what do you naturally do? What are you passionate about? What problems do you want to fix?

While input and insight are important to your identity and calling, it is vital that you seek what God has to say above everyone else's perception of you. God is filling in those broken, hurt, and discarded areas with His glory. I believe that so often, our giftings are found in the areas where we have received the most redemption, and therein lies our purpose.

NOTE

1. Wikipedia, "Kinstugi," accessed January 21, 2021, https://en.wikipedia.org/wiki/Kintsugi.

Birthday card from sister-in-law Andi, Summer 2015, right before pregnancy with firstborn David and before vision to move to California.

Jesse,

This is a significant year for you. A year of "NEW" + "FIRSTS". I sense that this year will bring renewal + multiplication in an exponential way. For relationships, salvation, & fertility. I sense Gods excitement over you, His absolute Joy + Pleasure as He watches you step into everything He has for you. You walk in humility in such a pure way and He will lift you up. Continue to submit your every plan to Him and He will make your path so obvious.

CHAPTER 6

Heart of Flesh

*Our error today is that we do not expect a converted man to be
a transformed man, and as a result of this error our churches
are full of substandard Christians. A revival is among other
things a return to the belief that real faith invariably produces
holiness of heart and righteousness of life.*
—**A.W. Tozer,** *Man: The Dwelling Place of God*

It was a warm afternoon in Orange County and I was driving to meet Parker and his brother for a BBQ. I buckled the boys into their car seats in the back of our Jeep Commander and put on "Salt of the Sound" radio on Spotify. I decided to take the scenic route from Costa Mesa to Seal Beach, which had me drive down the Pacific Coast Highway through Huntington Beach alongside the Pacific Ocean.

It's one of my favorite drives, and thankfully one that I get to do often. There's a point on the drive where the houses "disappear" and it's just the ocean on one side and marshes on the other. As I stopped at one of the traffic lights, I looked to the left and watched the sun slowly hiding itself behind the Pacific Ocean. One of the most beautiful things about California is the sunsets. I grew up on the East Coast and didn't realize that sunsets could look this way.

There is so much open sky in Huntington Beach that there can be an array of different paint strokes in the sky depending on where you're standing, where the sun is, and where you are looking. I closed my eyes for a brief moment and just whispered, "Thank You, Jesus, thank You that we get to live here."

As I reopened my eyes and looked at the road in front of me, I heard the Lord say to me, "Your heart of flesh is your greatest strength."

The words hit me, and they hit me hard. It was so clear that it was nearly audible. Tears welled up in my eyes as the Lord was ministering to me in my Jeep, on an ordinary night just meeting family for dinner.

"But what do You mean, Lord? What are You saying to me?"

I kept driving and whispering, "Lord, how do I keep a heart of flesh? What even is a heart of flesh?" I arrived at dinner and was pretty silent. Parker always knows something is up when I am not talking. The words seemed too precious, too sacred to share. After dinner, I pulled Parker aside as I loaded the kids back into the truck. I said to him, "Babe, God spoke to me on the drive over."

He replied, "That's awesome!" and then continued loading the stroller into the back of the Jeep.

The reality is, God speaks to me a lot, and I am so wildly thankful for the ability to hear His voice. I believe God longs to commune and reveal secrets to His people, if only we would ask. However, I knew that what the Lord had spoken to me on the drive had more "weight" on it. It was like a neon flashing sign saying, *"Pay attention!"* I didn't really understand what God was saying, but I knew I needed to spend time to press in. The next two years began a journey for me to discover what a "heart of flesh" is and why it would be so important for revival.

HAS YOUR HEART GROWN DULL?

Following that encounter with God, I spent several nights meditating on Matthew 13:11-15:

> *And he answered them, "To you it has been given to know the secrets of the kingdom of heaven, but to them it has not been given. For to the one who has, more will be given, and he will have an abundance, but from the one who has not, even what he has will be taken away. This is why I speak to them in parables, because seeing they do not see, and hearing they do not hear, nor do they understand. Indeed, in their case the prophecy of Isaiah is fulfilled that says:*
>
> *"'You will indeed hear but never understand, and you will indeed see but never perceive.' For this **people's heart has grown dull**, and with their ears they can barely hear, and their eyes they have closed, lest they should see with their eyes and hear with their ears and understand with their heart and turn, and I would heal them"* (ESV).

I am tearing up writing this because of how good God is. There is so much that He has in store for those who love Him. If I'm honest, I find it hard at times to minister in churches. I think about these words in Matthew 13, and it's hard for me to navigate the emotions I feel when I see people living deceived by religion rather than the full Kingdom life available. It's hard to be a preacher and hear someone tell me, "Great sermon!" and yet discern that they don't really understand. It feels so heavy at times.

Have we allowed our hearts to grow dull? Where have we compromised? Where have we allowed the enemy to deceive us?

Holy Spirit, I ask right now that You would shine a light on those areas and bring healing right now in the name of *Jesus!*

CUT TO THE HEART

I believe that to see ongoing transformation we need to allow God to keep our hearts raw, tender, and open to Him on a daily basis. I have discovered that one of the most important steps to prevent our hearts from becoming dull is to allow the Holy Spirit to access and heal any "stony bits." These are rough places that are stuck to the core of how we make decisions; they are attachments of pain, hurt, offense, and unforgiveness that don't belong in there.

I currently disciple three women—Taylor, Victoria, and Kendra. We do what our church calls "life on life" discipleship. This means that our discipleship goes beyond the scope of studying the Bible together in a program. We live life alongside one another. We cook meals together, share experiences, pray for one another, and study Scripture while trying to obey what it says.

There was one particular night we were chatting around my kitchen counter while I whipped up a tray of homemade eggplant parmesan (the girls' favorite!). As we started talking about relationships, Victoria became a bit defensive. I tease Victoria quite a bit, much like a little sister. When she got like this, I said, "Victoria, why are you acting crusty?" Crusty is the word we use when someone is being dismissive, hard, and defensive.

She looked at me from across the stovetop and said, "I don't know, but I can feel that I am." There was a deeper issue coming up to the surface that God was highlighting so He could heal it.

So often in self-help and church culture, we address the symptoms and not the core issue. Core issues take time, trust, and a process to heal and reveal.

For example, if someone on a church leadership staff has an affair, we address the affair. We usually remove them from staff (rightfully so), make sure the ramifications weren't too damaging to the congregation, and then send them to counseling for a "restoration process." We address the sin, but so often neglect what led to the sin.

The reality is, God is in the ministry of doing *deep* work. He wants to remove the "stones" attached to our hearts on the core level so that we can truly live free.

HIDDEN

As a young girl, I grew up going to the pumpkin patches on eastern Long Island with my mom. This quickly became an annual family tradition. We would load up the car and drive about an hour and a half to the local farms. Before "pumpkin picking" became a popular family outing, my mom would search diligently to find a farm where we could walk the fields and pick pumpkins right off of the vine.

I love picking pumpkins. However, I would be a fool to think that these pumpkins just "turned up." There is a farmer who, for the last year, has been working diligently for the harvest. He has tilled the soil, planted the seeds, and watered the ground. Now, the farmer does not have the ability to actually "create" a pumpkin. No, that is in the hands of God.

However, there is work that needs to be done for the miraculous harvest to happen.

That's how revival works in you and *through you.*

There's hidden work that's done. There are things God is doing in your life that are preparing you to steward the good things that He has in store. This process can feel brutal, lonely, and confusing. I feel like many in this season end up settling. They don't want to keep doing the secret hard work.

There's no "secret sauce" to making something like Saturate happen, but I have come to realize there is a *secret process.* There are many things that are done behind the scenes that create a framework for revival and for being the kind of person God can trust to lead others in revival.

Here's the truth: I didn't have any celebrity connections, megachurch endorsements, or preaching tours when I started Saturate. Every person I invited to come to preach turned me down for various reasons. I was on the roster to preach because everyone else could not come! I'm just Jessi Green who's obsessed with Jesus. I've spent years preparing sermons, even if I am only preaching to 20 people at the pier.

I believe that for many of us, we are in the "now" and "not yet" season of God's promises and prophetic words we have been given. We know there is more that God has for us, but we don't see it happening yet. This season can feel extremely frustrating. *Do not let your heart grow hardened!*

God takes us through a process in which He creates opportunities and allows trials to develop the internal heart needed for the things He has called us to do.

NUMB

When I was in labor with my son Ethan in September 2017, only half of my epidural was administered correctly. That means that half my body was completely numb, while the other half of my body was completely engaged in every contraction, painful transition, and exhausting push of labor. While my body entered into the stage of labor called transition, I screamed at the nurse to figure out a solution while sweat dripped down my face and my body was shaking. The truth is, it would have been far better to have had a completely natural childbirth than to have the pain and agony of a half-engaged body.

One of the most defining attributes of a heart of flesh is that it is beating full of life. We don't have to look far to see that so many in our world are half alive, numbed out, seeking to avoid pain. We overly medicate ourselves to treat anxiety and depression without pausing to go in deep and ask, "Why am I anxious? Where is this depression rooted?"

It surprises me how many believers have allowed their faith to be lulled asleep through apathy, distraction, or even pursuing comfort. So often, we can try to protect ourselves by "numbing out" and yet, by doing so, we miss the very life in front of us. I believe the Lord is allowing our current shaking to bring us back to life, like an alarm clock waking us up from our anesthetized slumber. God says in Revelation 3:15-16,19-20:

> I know your deeds, that you are neither cold nor hot. I wish you were either one or the other! So, because you are lukewarm—neither hot nor cold—I am about to spit you out of my mouth. …Those whom I love I rebuke and discipline. So be earnest and repent. Here I am! I stand at the door and knock. If anyone

hears my voice and opens the door, I will come in and eat with that person, and they with me.

Our Father, the one who knit us in our mother's womb says, "I am knocking." Has our apathy grown to the point where we can no longer hear the invitation from the Lord to wake up? Have our church attendance and church programs convinced us that God is satisfied with good note-taking and not big risk-taking? I pray that you would allow the Holy Spirit to show you any areas where you have "numbed out." These areas very well may be an indicator of where you are being called to prepare for battle.

FIND HEARTS OF FLESH

Do you know anyone whose heart is fully alive and on fire for the Lord? Is there anyone you look up to who displays the Kingdom life you seek? What qualities about him or her stand out to you?

I love reading the stories of late revivalists. Their zeal and consecration inspire me to burn! I feel encouraged at what is possible. I hold on to their testimonies as promises for what is possible, here and now.

As for those who are living, I deeply admire Heidi Baker. I have admired her ministry and life over the last ten years. To me, she is a great example of a yielded life, set apart and full of the love of Jesus. When she speaks, you truly believe that she knows God intimately, and she stokes a deeper hunger in those who will listen. Since I started truly following Jesus in my Manhattan apartment in 2009, all I have wanted is Jesus, the real Jesus. I wanted God to use me to share His love in power with a broken and hurting world. Heidi has reflected to me someone who knows *Him* personally. I want to be around people like that!

I have heard many people say flippant things like, "The same Holy Spirit who lives in Heidi lives in me," or, "Everyone is a revivalist."

While these statements might be true in theory, they neglect to mention the process that is involved. Sure, the same Holy Spirit who dwells in Heidi Baker, A.W. Tozer, Charles Finney, Kathryn Kuhlman, and more lives inside of you. The question is not whether or not you have received the same Holy Spirit. The question to ponder today is, how much of your life have you yielded to Him? How much of your life have you handed over to His Spirit to inhabit?

For years, I deeply pondered why it seemed like some people had a "special sauce" when it came to the Holy Spirit. After leading revival, I've discovered that God can do more *through* you as you step out of the way and allow His Spirit to take up full residency. For some of you, this may mean that you need to move and go find other burning ones. For others, you may need to leave your church where the congregation is "lukewarm" and submit yourself to leaders who are on fire and will lead you!

I believe that God is looking for hearts that are full of flesh, tender, and broken before Him. I believe He wants to pour out His love, miracles, revelation, and power on those who will submit to the process of removing the stony bits at all costs.

Having faith, when everything seems impossible, requires risk.

Choosing to trust, when you have been hurt and disappointed time and time again, requires a life laid down. Will you open up your heart to Him? Will you allow Him to remove the "crusty" corners where you have agreed that you will "never be hurt" again? Will you take a risk with me, to allow His Spirit to tenderize that old beating thing?

God is saying to you today, "I will give you a new heart and put a new spirit in you; I will remove from you your heart of stone and give you a heart of flesh" (Ezek. 36:26).

For how are we to live, if we have hearts of stone?

CHAPTER 7

The Gift of Repentance

*We all want progress. But progress means getting nearer to
the place where you want to be. ...If you are on the wrong
road, progress means doing an about-turn and walking back
to the right road; and in that case the man who turns back
soonest is the most progressive man.*
—**C.S. Lewis**, Mere Christianity

Jesus began His public ministry in Matthew 4:17 by saying, "Repent, for the kingdom of heaven is at hand" (ESV). This is a major instruction to revival with a promise attached to it. Here is another "blaze" for your journey. The Savior is telling us to turn away from our sins because the Kingdom realm is now an option for us and He knows that our sins will prevent us from accessing the Kingdom life, which is available now!

Scripture tells us that John was baptizing people in preparation for the Lord's coming:

> I baptize you with **water for repentance**. But after
> me comes one who is more powerful than I, whose
> sandals I am not worthy to carry. He will baptize

*you with the **Holy Spirit and fire**. His winnowing fork is in his hand, and he will clear his threshing floor, gathering his wheat into the barn and burning up the chaff with **unquenchable fire*** (Matthew 3:11-12).

In the Hebrew language of the Old Covenant, two words are used for the concept of repentance. These are:

1. Nahum—to lament, to grieve. This word is describing the emotions that are aroused when motivated to take a different course of action.

2. Shub—this word expresses a radical change of mind toward sin and implies a conscious moral separation from sin and a decision to forsake it and agree with God.

In the Greek language of the New Covenant, there are also two words used, which parallel the Hebrew meanings of the word *repentance*.

1. Metamelomai—to have feeling or care, concern or regret, which is akin to remorse.

2. Metanoeo—to have another mind, which describes that radical change whereby a sinner turns from the idols of sin and of self to God.

As we dive in deeper, into the meaning of repentance, we find that there is so much more to repentance than just simply praying once in church that God will forgive us of our sins.

REPENTANCE IS A LIFESTYLE

Over the years, I have learned the practice of daily repentance and how to incorporate it into my life as a follower of Jesus. I am so tired of hearing preachers say, "Ohhh no, here we go. We are going to talk about repentance—are you ready?"

Enough.

Seriously.

If we want to see revival, if we want to see nations transformed with the power and love of God, then we have to show people the truth about repentance.

Repentance isn't this big scary thing. It's a gift!

As I mentioned in the previous chapter, our hearts require deep work. Our minds need radical transformation. This can't be a one-time thing because we are *constantly* being told, sold, and molded to believe that the ways of this world are better and more real than Jesus and the Kingdom of Heaven. This is a lie.

REPENTANCE BRINGS US BACK

Repentance brings us back—back to the truth. Back to Him.

As we see in the Hebrew word *nahum*, when we repent we grieve deep in our spirit. We allow our hearts to be cut by His holiness. This cutting, this grieving, is what actually allows us to transform. Once we are saved, we need to go through the process of sanctification, being transformed more into the likeness of Jesus.

If you are not seeing change in your life, invite the Holy Spirit to reveal to you any sins that you need to turn from.

In the Hebrew word *shub*, we see that this invitation to repent is when we make the decision to say, "Hey, you know what, today I am not going to do whatever I want. Lord, what do You want me to do today?" It's when our minds change radically away from sin and begin thinking more Kingdom minded.

Sin is an idol.

When we repent, we declare that we don't want that idol in our life, no matter how important or comfortable it has become. We want Jesus instead, no matter the cost.

WHY REPENT?

God is waking up believers to be people who are transformed by Him and who demonstrate His love and power to the world. Repentance is a key element to opening up personal and city-wide revival. *Without repentance, the Church will never access the true life-giving relationship that Jesus offers us.*

Spending time with God can't just be a "good Christian habit." Spending time in His presence, allowing His kindness to lead you into repentance, is the *only* way you will see actual transformation in your life.

Pause.

I'm going to repeat this so it can really sink in.

If you want to see transformation, growth, and to live the life God created you for—you cannot skip time in His presence and live a lifestyle absent of repentance. The sacrifice of Jesus on Calvary makes it possible for us to come before a *holy God* in our mess, in our sin, and allow *His glory* to *change us* from the inside out.

You may not see immediate effects of spending time in God's presence and embracing a lifestyle of repentance, but the light of God is still shining through. Then one day, all of a sudden, you'll notice you have transformed into a radically different person. The effects of spending time with Him *will* eventually manifest.

If I looked back at my life a month ago, it may be hard for me to recognize much change in my life. However, if I look at how much God has molded and transformed me over the last ten years, I am left with a humble thankfulness for how much love, kindness, and healing the Lord has done.

FUTURE STARTS NOW

There is a section of Scripture that I often declare over myself when I feel discouraged. I can so easily become distracted by things in the world pulling for my attention, my admiration, my worship. In First Peter 1:3-5, I find the powerful *why* behind my lifestyle of repentance.

> *Because Jesus was raised from the dead, we've been given a brand-new life and have everything to live for, including a future in heaven—and the future starts now! God is keeping careful watch over us and the future. The Day is coming when you'll have it all—life healed and whole* (MSG).

Sometimes, I forget that Jesus is alive. I can turn on a sermon podcast in the car, listen to these awesome principles and teachings, and think about ways to live a better life and achieve my goals.

Friends, this is no different than picking up any New-Age or self-help book and applying it to your daily habits. If it's just a "good idea," you might see some minor change in your life, but you will certainly not access Heaven!

Peter is one of my favorite disciples (after John!). He is just a *little* intense and is *all* in—with everything. At one point, his faith faltered, he failed and denied Jesus, yet one moment on the beach with the *resurrected Jesus* reignited him to burn, burn, burn!

I can just imagine Peter saying to the early Christians, those who were scattered and being persecuted, "Hey, this is it! This is the real thing we have been waiting for. Jesus rose from the dead! He did it! That means we have a brand-new life, purpose, and we can enter Heaven. That Heaven realm isn't just for when you die; no, it's available now! Your new life, it starts today!"

When we are first converted to Christ, it is easy to repent of such obvious sins as drunkenness, stealing, hatred, not tithing, fornication, and so on. One encounter with God and we see how far we have gone from His original design. When I was saved in that dark bedroom, I hid under my covers in fear of seeing a holy God face to face. My sins, my lies, my secrets, the abortions, the stealing, the constant energy to keep up appearances—they didn't just grieve me. No, *grieve* is too light of a word. When I encountered God's peace in my bedroom, those sins—they tormented me.

No one had to convince me to repent.

I was lying in bed in awe. Could God, the living God, actually forgive me? Was He actually willing to remove the shame that kept me awake until sunrise and wrapped me in so much fear that I was afraid to sleep and be alone with my thoughts?

Ha ha! Amazing grace! Oh Church, we sing it, but have you experienced it? Repentance is easy, friends, when you have encountered the living God. It is also easy when you know fully well that satan, the one prowling like a lion, is looking for someone to devour and wants access to your life by one little compromise (see 1 Pet. 5:8).

Repentance that leads to revival is far beyond repentance of those obvious sins that we are so desperate to be freed from. Revival begins when a small group of yielded ones allow the Holy Spirit to search them and purify them in greater measure. Churches around the world see sinners ask for forgiveness of their sins and make a declaration to follow Jesus on a weekly basis. This isn't revival. This is normal Christianity.

Revival repentance is deeper.

It is all encompassing.

It's when we dare to ask the Holy Spirit to reveal to us *even the good things* that are preventing us from having full access to Him. It's when we ask God to show us the ways we have been prideful, ways that we would want to defend. It's when we ask for forgiveness mid-conversation because it sounds like gossip. It's when we remove a social media post because our heart behind it was passive-aggressive. It's when we turn down an opportunity that looks like promotion because our discernment feels like the agenda behind it is "off." It's when we give away things that we once held precious because they have taken up too much room in our hearts.

Yes, in the last year those are just a few of the real-life examples of revival repentance that I personally have had to experience. I am sure this is just the beginning. We are all being invited to go deeper still.

There is a simple daily practice that I started doing in 2016, and since then I have seen so much transformation happen in my life personally.

Every time I shower, I say a quick prayer: "Speak to me, Lord. Here I am. Search my heart. Is there anything that offends You?"

Then I pause.

I allow the Holy Spirit to speak to me as I silently shower.

If anything comes to mind, I ask for forgiveness. If something comes up that I want to "defend," then I ask the Holy Spirit to help me let go of that thing and to show me how it is damaging me and my future.

After I ask for forgiveness, then I pray: "God, show me what You are doing. I submit it all to You, once again. I'll do anything *You* tell me to do."

He has led me closer to Him every time.

I encourage you to make it a habit to ask God these same questions and to invite Him in a little deeper into your heart. Then, when He answers, simply respond to what He says.

KNOWING HIM

The harsh reality is, for a very long time I was in rebellion against God. I didn't know that I was in rebellion against Him, but I was deceived. I was deeply convinced that the world and the praise of people could offer me something better than God Himself.

As I sit on the plane writing this chapter, my fingers are trembling. I am so thankful, in a way, that I can distinctly remember the stale smell of my cold, dark apartment on 31st Street in Manhattan. I didn't even have a dresser in my bedroom at that point, my life was in chaos, and my clothes lay in piles on chairs next to my bed. I didn't want to pray, I didn't want to have alone time, and hearing from God wasn't on my radar. I didn't read books, I didn't create, I didn't rest. I filled every waking moment with new people, expensive luxuries, new experiences, and late-night cocaine conversations that went in circles and had no meaning.

I'm so thankful for the million trillion ways God has rescued me. It's so easy for me to obey God, to repent, to live for Him *because I know Him*. I am saying I really, really know and love God. We have a friend-ship. I trust Him more than anyone or anything. I am desperate to convince you that you can fully trust Him too.

This isn't just about changing the world; it's about the possibility of what could happen if *your* world is changed by really knowing Him. I think that could be the greatest supernatural miracle of all. Don't you agree?

Excerpt of *Lectures on Revival of Religion* by Charles Finney.

> And now, will you break up your fallow ground? Will you <u>clear your heart</u> before God as just pointed out and persevere until you are thoroughly awake? If you fail here, if you do not do this, you will <u>not get any further</u>. I have gone as far with you as possible until you renew your neglected spiritual life.
>
> Without a heart ready to receive the fullness of Jesus again, the rest of this book is worthless to the reader. It will only harden you and make you worse. If you do not start working on your heart immediately, one can say that you have no intention of being revived; and you have forsaken your minister, letting him fight the battle alone. If you do not do this, I charge you with having forsaken Christ, with refusing to repent and work for Him.

Wow, READ this after writing "Heart of flesh". Thank you Jesus!

CHAPTER 8

Relationship Status

That is one thing I am so afraid of: I am afraid lest I grieve the Holy Spirit, for when the Holy Spirit is lifted from me, I am the most ordinary person that ever lived.
—**Kathryn Kuhlman**

Have you ever had a complicated relationship before?

I was in college when Facebook released the "relationship status" feature and it was a very big deal. It was pretty much all everyone was talking about on campus at University of Miami. You'd walk into the library and hear, "Oh my gosh, did you see Kyle's relationship status?" "Wow, Katie is in a complicated relationship with Doug." As if in college you need more fuel to the gossip fire that spreads quickly through fraternity row, pillaging any helpless victim in its way.

I always wondered why someone would put on Facebook under relationship status, "It's complicated." If I am honest, it seems a bit awkward. Perhaps, for the internet, this is a bit "TMI" (too much information). If it's complicated, isn't that a signal that you should probably just end the relationship? Yet for some reason you now want complete strangers to understand your relationship troubles.

The reality is, it's inherent for us to figure out our relationship status with people. It's as though we can't help ourselves. We even do this with friendships. As I scroll through Instagram, I see comments like, "This is my tribe." It can all feel a bit complicated at times.

When I first started dating Parker, it was, well, complicated. As you could imagine, dating your pastor is one of the most complicated dating scenarios that could exist. I would not encourage any of you to wade into these murky waters! In 2013, Parker moved to New York City to lead the "Union Square" location of the church I attended. He was young, fit, attractive, loved God, and most important of all—single! As soon as Parker started leading, our church grew, especially in the female demographic. Girls would arrive to church early and save seats as close to the front row as they could, where Parker was sitting. It all felt a bit uncomfortable and desperate if you ask me. So, obviously, I decided that I would *not* like Parker.

One night at a friend's party, I said to my friend Gracie, "I don't like Parker; he's not even funny." She rolled her eyes at me and responded, "It's weird how often you bring up someone you don't like." I felt caught in my denial. Our church would host these things called "family dinners" after service, and I was usually in charge of organizing the group to go. One Sunday at family dinner, Parker came over to my table and asked, "Jessi, would you mind organizing a Monday night football party? You're a pretty social person."

I said, "Yes."

I hate football, but I agreed.

Then came this awkward lingering tension at the table. Parker just stood there, and I looked at him silently wondering if there was anything else. After a few moments, my friends and I gathered our things to head home. As I was walking down the stairs, he then said, "Okay, let's talk about this more. How can I reach you?" I gawkily replied, "I don't know…maybe by carrier pigeon?"

My face burned red hot as I rushed down the stairs while shouting out my phone number to the entire restaurant. Once outside, I whispered under my breath, "Why? Why did I say that? Just kill me now. Please erase that from your mind!" The entire subway ride home, Leah and Gracie mocked me as we collectively decided that any shot of me dating Parker was now officially over.

After about two months of group hangouts, small group, and "meetings" about possible venues for church, Parker made a *defining* move in our relationship. He "threw it out there" and tested the waters, like any skilled millennial Christian male. He texted me and said, "What does a girl like you want for Christmas?"

I thought to myself (and verbally processed about one million times to Gracie and Leah): "Okay…two situations here. Either A, he likes me or B, he's a creepy pastor who buys Christmas presents for everyone."

Luckily, it was not option B.

This back and forth banter went on for another long, agonizing winter month as we approached the holidays. I kept saying things to my friends like, "I think Parker likes me, but I don't want to really think that because if you're the girl in church who thinks your pastor likes you, you are weird. I don't want to speculate, and I don't want to make it awkward between us, but this is all so complicated. If he doesn't ask me on a date soon, I'm going to freak out."

Then, on December 10, I got the phone call that changed everything. I saw his name pop up on the screen of my phone and my hands began to sweat as I paced in my apartment, looking for a room to hide in away from my many roommates. When I picked up, he said, "Jessi, I have to tell you something."

I hesitantly responded, "Okay…"

Then he muttered out, "So, I had breakfast with my sister Andi this morning…" and I'm thinking in my head, *Okay, cool, good for you.* Then I continued to wait patiently on the other end of the phone during one of the longest pauses in all of history. Then Parker said, "I told Andi that I liked someone. Well, that person is you. Would you like to go out this Saturday?"

I said, "Yes." I then hung up the phone and ran around my apartment pounding on Gracie's bedroom door! "Gracie! We are going on a date this *Saturday*. It's happening. It's official. He likes me! I am not crazy!"

WHAT'S MISSING?

I wonder how many of us feel like we're in a complicated relationship with God. For years, this is what my Christianity felt like. It seemed more complicated than it should be. Throughout my teen years, I would see people share these "revelations" in the Bible. I'd hear people crying at youth conferences and I'd be thinking, *I'm not crying, the Bible is kind of boring, and are all of these people just full of it?*

> *This is how God showed his love among us: He sent his one and only Son into the world that we might **live** through him* (1 John 4:9).

John writes, "This is love: not that we loved God, but that he loved us and sent his Son as an atoning sacrifice for our sins" (1 John 4:10). Jesus died for us while we were His enemies. This is one of the hardest things for me to understand and probably one of the most provoking. You see,

God is making the "grand gesture" without a guaranteed response from us. He put it all "out there" while many of us were screaming, "I hate You, God." God's love is so wild, so radical, and so extreme that He's like, "I still love you. I will sacrifice everything for you, even when you hate Me."

God loved us first and is still loving us first.

He defined the relationship.

He took the first step. We did not. The word that John uses to describe this untamed love is the Greek word *agape*. You may have seen the word printed on some cheesy Christian T-shirts, but for many of us we have no idea what this word even means. The Greeks had to invent a word for this kind of love because it's not the kind of love you naturally have. This is the highest of the loves—divine love, or agape.

C.S. Lewis helps to define *agape* love for us:

> *Charity* means love. It is called Agape in the New Testament to distinguish it from Eros (sexual love), Storge (family affection) and Philia (friendship). So there are four kinds of love, all good in their proper place, but Agape is the best because it is the kind God has for us and is good in all circumstances.
>
> …Agape is all giving, not getting. …Giving money is only one way of showing charity: to give time and toil is far better and (for most of us) harder.[1]
>
> To love at all is to be vulnerable. Love anything, and your heart will certainly be wrung and possibly be broken. If you want to make sure of keeping it intact, you must give your heart to no one, not even to an animal. Wrap it carefully round with hobbies and little luxuries; avoid all entanglements; lock it up safe in the casket or coffin of your selfishness. But in that casket—safe, dark, motionless, airless—it

will change. It will not be broken; it will become unbreakable, impenetrable, irredeemable.[2]

LOVE CHANGES YOU

One Thanksgiving, my mom shared a revelation with me in the kitchen. This revelation completely changed my life because God kept reminding me of it over and over again. Do you know the main difference between John and every other disciple in the Bible?

I'll tell you. John calls himself, "The one Jesus loves." He actually writes in his Gospel letter about himself that he is "the one Jesus loves." He doesn't use his own name to explain who he is in the story. Instead, he knew if he referred to himself as "the one Jesus loves," the early listeners would know that it was him. We have sung it before in church: "You're a good, good Father. It's who You are, who You are, who You are. And I'm loved by You. It's who I am, who I am, who I am."

However, here's the thing. At the last supper, before Jesus was on His way to the cross, He had a little conversation with His closest disciples. In Matthew 26, Jesus was chatting with Peter, but all the disciples were there. He said:

> "Truly I tell you," Jesus answered, "this very night, before the rooster crows, you will disown me three times." But Peter declared, "Even if I have to die with you, I will never disown you." And all the other disciples said the same (Matthew 26:34-35).

We later read that Peter denied Jesus three times, just like Jesus said. Did you know that John was the only disciple at the cross with Jesus?

The only one.

His identity became, "I am the one who is loved by Jesus." Meanwhile, Peter's identity was based on what he could "do" for Jesus: "I won't deny you." Not until after the resurrection did Peter have the identity shift he needed.

John was loved by Jesus.

I believe that if you don't receive the love of Jesus as your identity, it will be impossible to fulfill your calling. I even will go so far as to say that it will be impossible to serve on a Sunday in your church without feeling bitter toward people if your identity isn't based in being loved by Jesus. Eventually offense will sneak in, like it always does. When your identity comes from *any* other outside source, you leave your soul wide open to be ransacked with bitterness and entitlement.

Did you know that it is actually easy to love other people when you know how loved you are? It changes everything. Generosity, obedience, revival, persecution, fear of man, hidden seasons, all of these become platforms for purification when your heart is set on being loved by God. Jesus loves you so much. Do you know that? Do you spend time with Him? Do you let Him tell you how much He loves you?

THE WORD OF GOD IS FOR YOU

When you read the Bible, I want to ask you to say to the Holy Spirit, "Holy Spirit, speak to me specifically. Show me how this Scripture applies to me because the Bible is full of promise. Fill me with revelation and teach me the Word."

These written words that make up the Bible are God defining the relationship with you. We don't read it out of obligation, but we read it because there's so much more that God offers us than just the surface scratch you receive in church. Let's shift our identity together!

Scripture talks about being transformed by the renewing of our minds. We have to be transformed. John didn't just get a new identity overnight. He walked with Jesus.

I believe that you need to choose to take a tiny step every day. Each day choose to agree more with God than the world. As you read the Bible, choose one verse and think about it all day. Spend time in His presence. Practice daily disciplines. It will transform you. This is a promise from God.

NOTES

1. C.S. Lewis, "To Mrs. Ashton: From Magdalen College, 18 February 1954," in *Letters of C.S. Lewis* (New York, NY: HarperCollins, 1988), 560-561.

2. C.S. Lewis, *The Four Loves* (New York, NY: HarperCollins, 1960), 155-156.

CHAPTER 9

The Uneaten Banquet

It is both a blessing
And a curse
To feel everything
So very deeply.
—David Jones

I n 2018, we moved into a beautiful house in Costa Mesa after living in Huntington Beach for two years. The house made more room for our growing family, had a big backyard where we could host church gatherings, and had an extra bedroom where Parker's parents could move in as they transitioned from New York to California.

One day as I looked up at the sky, I could hear the planes slowly flying overhead from John Wayne Airport. The house we rent is only a few miles away from the airport and just minutes from the highway, which makes it the perfect location for a family of missionaries. The air smelled sweet that afternoon. Perhaps it was from the budding orange blossoms on the large tree in our backyard. There was a peace that filled our house that afternoon. Do you ever have days like that? When it feels as though the earth has stood still for a moment to catch its own breath?

My sons played on the swing set on the creaky wood play yard that once belonged to the children of our landlord. I closed my eyes for a moment to just rest in the peace and warmth of the sun. As I inhaled the sweet air slowly, I saw an intense vision.

THE BANQUET

In the vision, there was an opulent banquet table. The table was made of hearty wood and stretched out across the room. On the table was a beautifully gem-adorned linen cloth, shiny gold candelabras with towering ivory candles, sparkling crystal ware, and it seemed as though the entire table was somehow filled with light. As magnificent as the adornments to the table were, they paled in comparison to the food on the table. I have never seen such brightly colored, extravagant fruit. My eyes immediately noticed the large gold bowl with the towering mountain of oranges. The color of the fruit almost looked like the sun peeking out over the horizon during an early morning sunrise. The fruit was almost hard to look at.

It took me a moment to notice anything else besides the adorned table in front of me, until I realized there were others in the room. Around the table stood all different kinds of people, young, old, short, tall, and a myriad of ethnic backgrounds. As I looked at each person, I noticed that they each were standing different distances from the table. Some were standing near the table, picking off a few grapes and biscuits here and there, while others were walking around the table a bit "indifferent" to the extravagance set before them. I noticed my hands were on the wood, and for some reason it seemed offensive to some.

Toward the end of the table, I noticed a very large, greasy-looking man. He was dressed in fine clothing, but it was ripped and the fabric lay shredded over his stomach. He was covered in stains from pomegranates and other bright-colored fruit. He held one of the brilliant oranges in his hand and took a bite, right through the peel. As his teeth sunk in like an anchor leaving the deck of a ship, the juice of the orange spilled down his hand and ran down his arm, leaving droplets of the fine juice on the floor. I was so disgusted by the image that I nearly missed the shadow of the women standing behind him. I barely noticed her; she looked pale and emaciated as she slowly moved forward with the grace of a ballerina on pointe. She knelt down and picked up the droplet of juice with her finger and licked it up.

I noticed, in what seemed like a fog, a small group on the farthest side of the table hold hands and courageously step closer, enjoying the fruit. The gluttonous man didn't notice because he was too engrossed in consuming and making sure that no one nearby touched what was "his."

ORANGE COUNTY

I opened my eyes and stared at my two boys pumping their legs on the swing set in our backyard as I tried to process what I just saw in the vision. It felt so weighty that I felt like if I tried to stand up, I'd come crashing back down onto the cement patio.

Sometimes, leading revival while raising three children under four years old is no easy task. I can find myself slip into self-pity at times when I see other ministers writing about spending all day in a vision, or traveling to minister in the third world on a whim, or seeing young moms at the beach, tanned and reading their books without a care in the world. Yet I'm out here wiping poopy diapers, sending emails to pastors till midnight, organizing tents, and ordering megaphones all while waking up at the crack of dawn to read my Bible and trying to process the deep, weighty visions God shows me while pouring orange juice into sippy cups.

Little side note: We don't have time for self-pity when God is answering our prayers. We can't allow the actions or opinions of others to make us feel insecure as we step into the big things God has for us.

As I made my kids lunch, I thought about how my children have full access to all of the food in our fridge. The orange juice is readily available for them; they simply need to ask. As I twisted the lids tightly onto the tops of the cups and handed them to David and Ethan, I thought about the emaciated woman. I asked the Lord, "Why did she only step forward for the spilled droplet of juice when the table was full of ripe fruit?"

No answer.

For months, I pondered the vision. There are elements still today that I don't fully understand. I couldn't get the picture of the edacious man out of my mind. There was a deep part of me that despised him. I knew in the vision that the Lord had prepared the banquet, that He had set it up to be enjoyed, and it seemed like the man was doing just that. Yet something felt off. Perhaps it was because he kept consuming for himself, while others around him starved.

Perhaps the banquet has always been set before us as something to be shared.

BANQUETS AND FEASTS

When the Lord shows you a vision, one of the first steps is to see if you can find clues that align with the Word of God. There are two prominent stories in the Gospels that are about banquets and feasts. I believe these two parables are significant for us as we step into the revival that is ahead.

The Parable of the Great Banquet is found in Luke 14:15-24. It is similar to the Parable of the Wedding Feast in Matthew 22:1-14, with a few differences.

Before the Parable of the Great Banquet, Jesus had just been teaching about the Kingdom realm to His disciples, healed a man, and was dining with the recognized religious leaders of the day. Many of the prominent leaders sitting at the table would subscribe to the idea that only the Jews could partake in the Kingdom realm. When Jesus mentioned the resurrection, someone at the table with Him said, "Blessed is the one who will eat at the feast in the kingdom of God" (Luke 14:15). In reply, Jesus shared the Parable of the Great Banquet:

> *A certain man was preparing a great banquet and invited many guests. At the time of the banquet he sent his servant to tell those who had been invited, "Come, for everything is now ready."*
>
> *But they all alike began to make excuses. The first said, "I have just bought a field, and I must go and see it. Please excuse me."*
>
> *Another said, "I have just bought five yoke of oxen, and I'm on my way to try them out. Please excuse me."*
>
> *Still another said, "I just got married, so I can't come."*
>
> *The servant came back and reported this to his master. Then the owner of the house became angry and ordered his servant, "Go out quickly into the streets and alleys of the town and bring in the poor, the crippled, the blind and the lame."*
>
> *"Sir," the servant said, "what you ordered has been done, but there is still room."*

*Then the master told his servant, "Go out to the roads and coun-
try lanes and compel them to come in, so that my house will be
full. **I tell you, not one of those who were invited will get a
taste of my banquet"** (Luke 14:16-24).*

VIP ACCESS

I've probably read that banquet parable nearly 100 times, yet God
was revealing something new to me in this season. In my early 20s, I
worked in the nightclub industry for five years and deeply understood
the meaning behind an invitation. The more prestigious the host, the
more exclusive and coveted the guest list becomes.

There was one particular club in Miami called "Mansion" where I
worked during my senior year of college. My job was to work with the
doorman on the VIP lists and make sure all those who were VIPs were
given priority. You see, if a celebrity or famous athlete reserved a table, he
would request certain names to be put down on his list. This list guaranteed entry and special access. Those on the list could skip the long line,
have free drinks, and be escorted to a table behind the coveted velvet
rope into the VIP section.

Now, let's say Zack the real estate agent wanted to get in. Zack usually had three options available to him:

1. Be on the VIP list of a celebrity or promoter.

2. Spend a few thousand dollars on bottle service.

3. Show up with 10 or more supermodel-looking girls and no
   other guys and tip off the doorman and hope to get in.

I always felt sorry for groups of guys traveling from out of town who would show up at the nightclub door. They were all so excited to go in, dance the night away, and possibly meet a new love interest. *These guys always got denied.* I hated this part of the job because I hated seeing the disappointment fall on their faces. They would wait for hours in the line, negotiate, offer hundreds of dollars, and still be denied. It wasn't really their fault; it was the fault of the industry. Nightclubs have societal rules if they want to stay open and be successful. *Exclusivity.* Curated crowds. A greater female to male ratio. I could keep going. The rules are what provide the feeling of "status" for those who enter. That feeling is worth tens of thousands of dollars per night. The nightclub industry is a dealer of that feeling.

I'm so thankful for my years working in the night-club industry. While there were many dark days, I learned some important lessons for revival, another "blaze" on your journey. *When you are given an invitation of great value, you prioritize it.*

When I got saved, I realized deep within my soul that I was being given the greatest invitation. Not only was I being given access to the Kingdom, I was being given VIP access to the King Himself. He was inviting me, with all of my brokenness and pain, to a seat at *His* VIP table.

As I learned to sit with Him and enjoy His presence, He gave me the greatest honor on earth. He invited me to be His trusted "Kingdom promoter." He told me that my job was to invite everyone and anyone to come and enjoy VIP access, that my days of rejecting others (out of fear of rejection myself) were over. I now was given the rubber stamp of *approval* and could stamp VIP onto every hand that crossed my path. This is an honor I have not taken lightly. I couldn't wait to see the expression on so many people's faces as they were given entry to the very thing their hearts had been created for! What surprises me, over the last ten years, is who has responded to the invitation and who has not.

Here is the problem—that repulsive greedy man at the end of the table in my vision, the one with orange juice dripping down his plump arms—he smirks at me with the lacerated orange peels between his teeth. I finally know who he is and why he repulses me to the core. He's that old spirit that we all think has no control over us while we stand back starving for life, lapping up droplets of juice like beggars at our own Father's banquet. He's the one that makes you push everyone out of the way so that you can "get *your* miracle, just one more impartation!" I've watched in horror as the children of God plead the miracle-working preacher to feed their starving souls. That old spirit, he is the one blocking you from the peace, the breakthrough, the *daily* encounter in His presence. He's the one that will work you to the bone, slaving away for your identity.

Ah, you know exactly who I am talking about, because that gluttonous spirit rules powerfully here in America. He is the spirit of religion. He is the one whose fat body is blocking entrance into revival for every one of the saints. The thing is, he has become too engorged with himself. He's become so consumed with himself that all he can do is mock or try to convince you that you "need him" in some sick, perverted way. So you see, if you simply decide to push past him and come to the table, there is absolutely nothing he can do to stop you! I say, come.

> *The Spirit and the bride say, "Come!" And let the one who hears say, "Come!" Let the one who is thirsty come; and let the one who wishes take the free gift of the water of life* (Revelation 22:17).

PART 3

Tools for the Field

*Young converts should be taught that they have **renounced the ownership of all their possessions, and of themselves, or if they have not done this they are not Christians**. They should not be left to think that anything is their own; their time, property, influence, faculties, bodies, or souls. "Ye are not your own;" all belong to God; and when they submitted to God, they made a free surrender of all to him, to be ruled and disposed of at his pleasure. They have no right to spend one hour as if their time was their own. No right to go anywhere, or do anything, for themselves, but should hold all at the disposal of God, and employ all for the glory of God. If they do not, they ought not to call themselves Christians, for the very idea of being a Christian is to renounce self and become entirely consecrated to God. A man has no more right to withhold anything from God, than he has to rob or steal. It is robbery in the highest sense of the term.*

—Charles G. Finney, Lectures on Revivals of Religion,
"Instructions to Converts"

CHAPTER 10

Living Spirit Led

If the presence of God is in the church, the church will draw
the world in. If the presence of God is not in the church, the
world will draw the church out.
—Charles G. Finney

In 2019, I personally emailed over 100 churches in Orange County to partner and participate in Saturate. The Lord told me that there would be a great harvest, that He was answering the prayers of His people. He told me, "Jessi, do not worry about outcomes. Your job is simply to create the space and invite people to the banquet of My Kingdom." He said, "Summer 2020 is the beginning of the harvest."

I researched for weeks and emailed and invited local pastors over for a special dinner at our house. Parker woke up at 3 a.m. to smoke a brisket for 14 hours. We wanted to honor these leaders with a great meal, as we shared with passion what the Lord was showing us for Southern California.

Parker and I are unknown in Orange County. We are "younger" in ministry, don't lead a megachurch, and are really new to the region. Many of the leaders in the area had been a part of the Jesus People movement in the '60s and '70s in Southern California. They have been praying for revival to come again for 40 and 50 years. I wasn't really quite sure why God had even called us here. Couldn't we be of better use for the Kingdom somewhere else, somewhere with fewer "Christians"?

The first year we moved to Orange County, we would meet for coffee with Bob Fulton, who helped pioneer the Vineyard Church movement alongside his brother-in-law, the late John Wimber. As he shared, we leaned in as his heart felt heavy regarding the lack of discipleship in the church movements of the past. We clung to every lesson and experience he had with regard to why the Jesus People movement came to an end.

On a random afternoon, while reading my Bible outside of a bakery, Stan Frisbee randomly gave me a prophetic word about an evangelistic anointing I carried. He is the brother of the late Lonnie Frisbee, who many believe pioneered the Jesus People movement. These carriers of revival are just walking the streets of Orange County, dishing out prophetic words!

Parker and I were invited to small worship gatherings at Blaine Cooke's house. We attended his house for a year without a clue who he was. Then one summer afternoon, I read in *Defining Moments* by Bill Johnson that Blaine is the one who led healing services with the Vineyard and also laid hands on Randy Clark who in turn catalyzed the Toronto Blessing. I looked at Parker in the pool one day and said, "This can't possibly be the same Blaine whose house we have been going to?!" It was as though the impartation for revival, to pick up where the Jesus People movement dropped off, was chasing us down! Parker was a bit of a skeptic to the "charismatic supernatural" until Blaine, one summer evening, laid hands on him to receive the power of God, which left Parker shaking on the floor.

There is no short supply of stories of God's goodness here in Orange County. Many have witnessed great revival and, with eager hearts, begged the Lord to "do it again." We have noticed that since 2016, many

Spirit-filled leaders have "ended up" in Southern California, unsure of their assignment, simply responding obediently to a call from the Holy Spirit to "come."

In spring 2019, I heard the Lord say, *"Green light, the harvest is summer 2020."* So, as you can imagine, it was with great eagerness and excitement that I reached out to as many pastors and leaders as I could to tell them the good news! The Lord had heard their prayers; He was bringing in the harvest!

PLANS

For our first dinner with the pastors in the region, we had about 40-plus leaders in our home. I was surprised by how many people did not respond or expressed a lack of interest, but was thankful that we still gathered this many leaders in our home. With great zeal, I shared what I saw with every leader, as they chewed down their smoked brisket. In 2016, during prayer and fasting, I had a vision of people being baptized in Huntington Beach. In the vision, there were so many people that it felt chaotic. People were turning around to baptize the person behind them in a flurry. I shared how we needed the churches in Orange County to unify. We needed to mend the nets and prepare to disciple the incoming harvest. The Lord had said "The next revival will be the equipping of the saints."

Our plan was to host a three-night conference that would train and inspire people to share the Gospel. We would give them practical tools and baptize them in the Holy Spirit. We would plan the event on the same weekend to coincide with the US Open of Surfing in Huntington Beach. It was a great plan! Tens of thousands come to the beach to watch that competition. It would be *there* that we would leave our comfortable rows *in* the church and *go out* and share the Gospel and *be* the Church. We would baptize people *en masse*, then come back to the venue and worship together. I was very excited for our "outreach focused" conference called "Saturate OC." This was my "solid" plan to win the lost in Orange County!

From this regional vision-casting meeting, and about 50 other coffee meetings, lunches, and phone calls through 2019 and into 2020, we had confirmed around 25 church partners to come together to make Saturate's "conference" happen. I was ecstatic—this was no small feat! Our weeks were filled with emailing, calls, meetings, and lunches with pastors. I shared the vision and plan so many times, I could share it in my sleep. We had a few of the "big" churches on board and made many friends in the process. We found that most churches we met with could get on board with the "evangelism conference" and could all agree that their members needed to share the Gospel. I was still a bit disheartened by the churches and movements that seemed unresponsive, yet I remained faithful to my mandate to continue to invite and create space for people to partner. I kept telling myself, "Stay humble, be the persistent widow."

We soon gathered a committee of Spirit-filled believers we would meet with monthly to pray, plan, and coordinate efforts. As I planned, I kept hitting one wall after another. One issue is that I could not find a speaker for the event. (I could write a whole chapter about this!) We invited nearly every popular evangelist you could think of. Every single one was either already booked, on vacation during that time, or simply didn't respond. I didn't know who was going to speak, and I was on my hands and knees begging the Lord to give us one speaker for the event! During one of our committee meetings, as we decreed over California the promises of God, Pastor Doug Healy looked across the room and said, "Jessi, you are supposed to speak. You are at the center of God's eye."

I recorded the whole prophetic word as he and his wife Debbie prayed in agreement that God was raising me up in this hour. However, my insecurities and fears continued to rise. "No one knows who I am, no one is going to come if I speak." My journal pages were filled with prayer requests. "Lord, we need a speaker! God, help us find a venue!"

CHANGE

In March 2020, a major shift happened to our plan. After spending five months applying for beach permits, being denied, looking for venues, and reaching out to churches, I finally settled on the conference space at the Hyatt in Huntington Beach that was directly across the Pacific Coast Highway and only a short walk from the pier. The week before I was about to sign a $30,000 contract (with only $15,000 in the Saturate bank account!) to book their conference space, California announced it would be entering into a two-week "lockdown" to flatten the curve for the worldwide pandemic of COVID-19. Everything was essentially being shut down. The world waited (without toilet paper and limited food supplies) as we lived in limbo, learning about a virus that seemed to be sweeping the globe and filling our hospitals and social media news feeds.

My husband and I (now 30 weeks pregnant)—along with our two children at the time, my in-laws Bob and Mavis, and our friends Kendra and Victoria—decided to go up to Kern River and stay in our RV trailer to unplug and wait out the chaos, unmasked, as we skipped rocks alongside the riverbeds. Churches and ministries closed their doors with not many other options to gather except online. We all opened webinar accounts, and many of us learned how to livestream for the first time. It worked—for a while. I kept checking the news, refreshing my feed, waiting and seeking updates about when life would go back to "normal." Two weeks turned into over a month as I tossed and turned on our thin RV mattress while approaching my due date and getting larger by the day. Tears rolled down my cheeks as my baby shower was cancelled and I witnessed friends and family shut down their businesses, postpone weddings, and wait, and wait, and wait.

When the Olympics announced that they would be "postponing" to 2021, I knew that things were looking dim for Saturate's conference. I emailed the Hyatt, and they regretfully informed me that they still had no updates on when they would be reopening and able to host any events. I sat with Parker near our campfire and said to him, "Parks, we have to reschedule Saturate, right? Everything is cancelled."

He then glanced up at me and said, "What has God told you?"

I rolled my eyes and responded, "Nothing. That's the most frustrating part. He has literally told me nothing."

I went back into the RV, tired, cold, and over camping. Over it all. I was sick and tired of planning Saturate, making a plan, then having to change that plan. I was emotionally done. If anything, COVID was the greatest excuse to postpone until 2021. Everyone would understand, it would give me an additional year to plan and bring in more partners, and I could take this summer to rest. Self-pity began to sneak in. I had never had the chance to have a maternity leave with any of our other children. The Lord "made me" move to California when our firstborn David was only two months old. I had worked so hard and deserved to just rest and be with our third baby. It was settled—I would postpone to 2021! This made perfect sense—I'd have more time to search for venues, solidify speakers, and get more registrations and no one would think it was weird!

THE OTHER SIDE

The next morning, I woke up and read the Gospel of John. I was reading the story of Jesus appearing to His disciples after the resurrection. I read in John 21:3-6:

> *"I'm going out to fish," Simon Peter told them, and they said, "We'll go with you." So they went out and got into the boat, but that night they caught nothing.*
>
> *Early in the morning, Jesus stood on the shore, but the disciples did not realize that it was Jesus.*
>
> *He called out to them, "Friends, haven't you any fish?"*
>
> *"No," they answered.*
>
> *He said, "Throw your net on the right side of the boat and you will find some." When they did, they were unable to haul the net in because of the large number of fish.*

After I read these words, I felt the Spirit say to me, "It's time to throw your net on the right side of the boat. California hasn't seen another revival because they are stuck in 'old ways' of what once worked. Keep your eyes on the man on the beach (Jesus) and you will catch a great harvest. *I did not lie when I said the harvest begins summer 2020, and I am not surprised by COVID-19."*

I knew at that point that Saturate would not be cancelled or postponed; it would just look different from what we expected. But what did it mean to "throw the net on the other side"?

April 15th 2020

I sense God wanting to stretch my faith. I feel like I'm at the end of myself. On Easter, I broke down — questioning if all of this is real + worth it. I'm tired of not seeing the kingdom manifest around me, telling others stories, reading more books but <u>no</u> power! I cant <u>do</u> another Christian Hype conference. I cant gather people though promotion. God, either you are with me or you are <u>Not</u>! I'm reading 4th dimension and wanting to live a life of miracles. 7,000 ppl got saved online though Greg Laurie — we <u>Are</u> in a revival. Lord, help open our eyes. I cant plant more churches or conferences though strategy. I bought Heidi Bakers workbook to live miraculously. God — I want the kingdom life <u>YOU</u> promised us.

Saturate OC options :

Current plan

A) 1 Day Activation event Aug 1st — go teams + Baptism Service $15K

@ Hyatt (emailed to negotiate rate to BISK)

4 Fridays Revival meetings @ Tower 20

Through August
- Baptize in Holy Spirit + Water
- Worship
- open to public

B) 2 day Activation event @ Rock Harbor Costa Mesa

July 3rd — (more conference style - worship, message, repentance)

July 4th — Go Teams (train @ Rock harbor, shuttle to beach)
5pm Baptism
6:30pm Beach Party

C) 2 day event @ Rock Harbor

July 31st — Aug 1st
Same style as plan B → end Sat night @ beach
4 Friday Revival meetings @ Tower 20

D) No big event
4 Friday Revival Nights @ Tower 20

AN INSIGNIFICANT PLACE

After a few weeks, we left camp and headed back to Orange County, while everything remained in "lockdown." We emailed our church partners that Saturate would still be happening, although we were coming up with a new "plan." Parker and I walked the beaches as I begged the Lord to reveal to me what would be the "right side of the boat."

For weeks, I heard nothing.

While I was 39 weeks pregnant, Parker and I drove down the Pacific Coast Highway on a misty morning. I cried out to the Lord, "What do I do? Where do we gather?" He highlighted to me "Lifeguard tower 20." Again, it made no sense to me. Any crowds (if at all) would be near Huntington Beach Pier. Lifeguard tower 20 was at least a 15- to 20-minute walk from Main Street. It seemed to me to be an inconvenient and insignificant location, but I said, "Yes."

Parker and I sat by the lifeguard tower and prayed and felt a peace about moving forward. I then felt the Lord urge me to move the dates from the end of July (when the US Open of Surfing was originally scheduled to be) to July 3, and to schedule four consecutive Friday nights through the month of July. Again, I could not make sense of the plans. July 3 seemed to be the worst night to launch a revival event. Many people travel on Fourth of July weekend, and I hesitated in fear that no one would show up.

The next week, I gave birth to our daughter, Summer. I decided to take two weeks off from my phone to just be present with my new baby, pray, and rest. As I held my tiny daughter swaddled in my arms, I saw a vision of a groundswell. I believed that the Lord was telling me to build expectation through prayer, training, and online teaching.

As we approached June, the plans and event had shifted so many times that it no longer looked remotely related to the original vision. I think that is the best thing that could have happened. After many emails from churches "backing out but still encouraging us," around eight churches remained partnered, with their leaders and about 400-plus believers signed up for a common mission. Through COVID-19, something significant shifted the partnership that we were not aware of. The original partnership around the "vision to equip the body of believers in evangelism through Saturate" became a *united* vision to worship Jesus on the beach, share the Gospel, and *be* the Church despite any circumstances. Those who remained, we were united, for a moment. For some, the unity was birthed out of fear of the government gaining too much control; for others it was out of a deep hunger to see God move. Either way, groundswell was developing.

The lessons that make you A Revivalist:

5/13/20

This whole thing with Saturate is completely messing w/ my identity + control. I feel soo weird - like why is God not just having me do a conference. Why must I always pioneer. Even re: registrations - its scary and I'm afraid of looking stupid. What _if_ no one comes!? I'm afraid of looking foolish - I'm afraid of not having it all togeather. I know that God is wanting intimacy — I want security!

Also - I'm tired of everyone being all talk / No Action!

SHUTDOWN

On July 2, the governor of California announced that he would be shutting down all beaches for the Fourth of July to avoid the spread of the virus. I texted several friends and the Saturate team to pray. Huntington Beach city council announced an emergency meeting and as a city decided that they would remain open July 3 and shut down on July 4. This was crazy! The beach would remain open just long enough for the first night of Saturate, despite the governor's orders!

That evening, I went to our friends Pete and Patti Shambrook's house for prayer. They had been hosting prayer nights every Thursday, and I knew I needed to be in the presence of God and among faith-filled believers. The group surrounded me in prayer, prophesying over what God was going to do, encouraging me to move forward and that God was with me. We had gotten so many emails from people asking if we were cancelling, and I whispered to the Lord, "I'm afraid. I am afraid of being humiliated, God. What if no one shows up?" I then heard Him say, "You show up. Keep creating space and don't worry about the outcome. I am with you always."

I texted Patti, Lauren, Tracy, Joanne, Chris, Tami, and Cathy. They are some of the most Spirit-filled women I know in Orange County. (Find other burning ones!) They prayed for me, encouraged me, and Patti said, "Jessi, no matter what, we will be there."

On July 3, I approached Tower 20 at 5 p.m. to help with setup. We had a simple neon yellow beach tent, two battery operated megaphones, and a small table with hoodies and towels available. I asked the Lord to show us a sign or wonder this evening that He was with us. Upon arrival, there were about 30 people on the beach, setting up, praying, and walking around. I invited my friends Melody Hernandez and Michael

Ketterer to lead worship that evening. Melody Hernandez informed me that the worship team had many issues come up that week, and they had to end up replacing many people in the band. At 6:15 p.m., we began to worship. With no amplified sound, no signs, no stage, and no lights, *hundreds began to gather on the beach.*

I shared a message about "are you really living?" and the vision of what the Lord was doing in Orange County. I talked about why we should share the Gospel and the many thoughts the Lord has about us. I had every person pick up a grain of sand to represent each thought He has for us and that when we give a prophetic word we are simply asking God for one grain of a thought of the many He has for that person. I then preached the Gospel of the death and resurrection of Jesus and invited the crowd into repentance. To my surprise, many people raised their hands to begin following Jesus. We invited them to come into the ocean to be baptized. The sea roared with large, violent waves like I had never seen. People hesitantly entered the waters while the oceans whipped the shore. People spontaneously decided to be baptized and the crowd cheered as the sun set along the beach.

That evening, many were delivered of demonic strongholds while they went down into the water. We prayed for people to be baptized in the Holy Spirit, and people were set free from depression, anxiety, and suicidal thoughts. Backs were healed, fingers were put straight, and the Lord moved powerfully. My soul burst with excitement; I knew we were on the cusp of a great revival.

That night, the news reported that the beaches in Orange County were hit with something they called a "King's Tide" that had flooded the beach, even into the streets. The streets were "saturated." It was the wonder and sign that I needed.

Psalm 139

With everything happening in culture, I believe you
are setting us up for a great Revival.
We see what you do + respond.
One, step, at a time
Fully yielded fully present
Holy Spirit Come! Fill us with your love!

→ every beach is closed but HB
All things to do are cancelled, restaurants re-closed
3 days before Saturate. You have consecrated this
space + time for Harvest.
Jesus → why me? Why did you call me from NY?
what do you have planned? Why not
someone else?
Thank you for taking your time with me.
For purifying my heart. For the wrestle.
I much rather lead a Revival than a conference —
thank you God that you know my heart!

Psalm 92

You _thrill_ me Lord with all that you have
done for me.

CHAPTER 11

The Church Has
Left the Building

In Huntington Beach, a revival with church at the ocean's edge.
—LA Times, *July 11, 2020*

The next few weeks felt like I was in a dream. I had a hard time navigating what was real, what was prophetic, and what was actually happening in front of me. The vision the Lord had given me in 2016 of thousands gathering on the beach and being baptized in Huntington Beach was really happening! As we approached the second week of Saturate, we were hit with *heavy* resistance. Our Instagram account was flooded with thousands of comments vilifying us. I opened up my email inbox to find hundreds of emails of praise *and* criticisms. People demanded answers as to how we could be "so reckless and not love our neighbors by wearing masks."

The governor then announced that churches could no longer worship together. This was the very fuel the revival fire needed. It ignited something in the backbone of the believers. Something the sleeping Church in America needed. CNN reported:

While you can still attend in-person church services in California, you can't sing. The state, *to curb a rapidly worsening pandemic*, has temporarily banned singing and chanting in places of worship.

"Practices and performances present an increased likelihood for transmission of Covid-19 through contaminated exhaled droplets and should occur through alternative methods like internet streaming," the state's Department of Public Health announced in an order Wednesday.

…Singing at services has proven to be one way to spread a virus, according to the Centers for Disease Control and Prevention.

The agency studied how coronavirus spread from one member to 87% of the singers at a Washington choir practice and said in a report:

"The act of singing, itself, might have contributed to transmission through emission of aerosols, which is affected by loudness of vocalization."

While the California Department of Public Health strongly recommends places of worship should continue to facilitate remote serves, in-person services are currently permitted in California if proper measures are followed.

Among the existing protocols, all houses of worship are required [to] limit their attendance to 25% of building capacity or a maximum of 100 attendees, the order says.[1]

Fall 2019, we had invited Sean Feucht from Bethel Church to lead worship at our original "Saturate Conference." I personally had never heard him sing, but my friend Tracy believed that as a former missionary he carried the passion we needed for our evangelism event.

He was excited and on board. He let us know that he was running for Congress, and his attendance at the event was conditional on if he made it through the primaries. We understood. He ended up not being elected as a congressional candidate and was going to be moving forward with us during the Saturate event. He and his team remained flexible as the event changed over and over again. The week we had scheduled Sean to lead worship with us on the beach was the same week that the governor announced that singing and worship was banned. In response, Sean launched a counter protest called "Let Us Worship."

The second week of Saturate OC beach revival meetings, Sean led worship and I preached the Gospel. Hundreds made decisions to follow Jesus, get baptized, and be filled with the Holy Spirit. Miracles, deliverance, and healing broke out. The LA Times reported:

> There's a revival taking place on the sand at Huntington Beach.
>
> On Friday, at least 200 evangelical Christian faithful gathered near lifeguard tower 20 to hear the word and be motivated to spread it. They sang and raised their hands skyward in praise. Several walked into the cool waves of the Pacific to be baptized at sunset.
>
> Three girls, best friends from a youth group at Influence Church in Anaheim Hills, waded into the water together to be baptized, again.
>
> "Someone came up and prayed for me and I felt like God spoke to me and I thought, why not?" said Bridgette Mayse, 16.

Annika Miller, 17, said dipping into the sea again was for her "a reawakening of boldness."

With the continuing coronavirus pandemic, traditional indoor church services have been interrupted or reimagined, either voluntarily or by government decree. On the beach, there were no pews or steeple. Gulls and paragliders soared overhead instead.

The seaside outreach movement is called Saturate OC and co-organizer Jessi Green calls it a "ripple-effect" revival, not one led by a single preacher.

Hundreds gathered for the weekly Saturate OC worship event north of the pier in Huntington Beach on Friday. They came to Huntington's shore to feel the spirit, and, as it is written in 2 Corinthians 3:17, and Green started to recite and the crowd enthusiastically filled in, "where the spirit of the Lord is there is freedom."

Radley Arnold, 25, was in town from Kansas to visit his girlfriend, who wanted to take him to service on the beach. Worship is all the more important during the pandemic, he said, with its restrictions on gatherings.

Arnold has been studying Christianity but wasn't planning to get baptized that evening. A preacher called out for people who wanted to go to the water, and he then felt the urge to stand. "I feel completely different," Arnold said, his wet hair glistening.

Green said she and her husband moved to Orange County from New York after having a vision of a mass baptism at the Huntington Beach Pier while here on vacation. Saturate OC draws together several local ministries for its outreach.

They were there last Friday too, and will return on the remaining Fridays in July. They hope to draw 2,000 disciples who can fan out to bring in 50,000 believers.

"The church," Green called into a microphone to cheers, "has left the building."[2]

Each week, the crowds increased. We witnessed more people say "Yes" to following Jesus, while our friends provoked them to enter into the water to be baptized and forgiven of their sins. Our friends, Pete and Patti and Cathy Greer, quickly organized a ministry team and trained nearly a hundred people to prophesy over others, cast out demons, and pray for the sick to be healed. It was as if Orange County was in supernatural revival bootcamp!

@cancelJessiGreen

As salvations increased by the hundreds each week, so did criticisms. Any given Saturday, I'd turn on my phone to find hundreds of emails asking how to get connected to a church, where the next baptisms were, and on the flipside hundreds were calling me a murderer and a cult leader. I think sometimes people forget that there is a person on the other side of the screen. A petition was created to shut us down and was submitted to the city council. My personal social media accounts flooded with testimonies, videos, and so many insanely good reports, and yet as I'd scroll down I'd find hundreds of comments tearing apart my character, our churches, and even my children. Fake accounts were created called @cancelJessiGreen and more. Victoria ended up having to take over the Saturate social media, while Joanne and Tracy took over the

Saturate email account to help me guard my mind from the curses and accusations.

Going into the "last" and fourth Friday of our Saturate beach gatherings, I could feel something shifting spiritually. It felt like an intensity was increasing. We spoke to Parker's parents, and they agreed that we should stay in a hotel that evening to "get off the grid" and pray and have some alone time as a couple. We checked into our hotel on Thursday evening, put our bags on the bed, and Parker's phone began to ring. It continued to ring, which is unusual, and Parker saw an unrecognized number. About an hour later, he received an email from the Huntington Beach city events manager. The email explained that we could not gather and that it was a state-wide violation of public health. The phone rang again, and Parker picked it up. The city events manager and the fire marshal were on the other line. I paced in the hotel and prayed while Parker went back and forth regarding our first amendment rights to assemble, how we were gathering outdoors, and so on. The call ended with the city manager saying, "Am I clear that you will not cancel?"

Parker responded with a resolute, "Yes, you are clear."

At that moment, we turned off our phones and began to pray. I took a warm shower and asked the Lord to reveal to me what He was doing. I felt like we were supposed to move forward with hosting additional weeks of revival on the beach, and yet there was so much opposition! I prayed in tongues throughout the night and hardly slept that evening. I woke up early, poured myself a cup of coffee, and sat on the balcony that overlooked Huntington Beach Pier.

I jotted quickly in my journal everything I was hearing: *waves, tsunamis, wildfires, fires up the coast, Nehemiah, Deborah...* "If we can't share the Gospel on the beach, then where can we go?"

Earlier that week, as I scrolled on Instagram, God highlighted Tim Manigault to me to help lead worship at Saturate that Friday with OC

Worship Nights and our dear friend Tommy Murphy. Although we had never met Tim, I quickly sent him a direct message, and he rearranged his schedule and said, "Yes!"

As I journaled and watched the sunrise, the Lord said, "Have Tim sing the song 'Tremble.' This will create a line in the sand."

I then heard God say, "If not now, then when? Tonight—many people are going to be saved. Many church attendees are going to follow Jesus. Send people to *go* and Saturate their city!"

That evening, we headed back to our house to see the kids, shower, and get ready for the night ahead. I nursed our two-month-old baby Summer on the bed while Parker quickly jumped in the shower. It was about 4 p.m. and we were leaving in an hour to head to the beach.

Our bedroom door was slightly ajar, and I heard a knock on the front door of our house. Parker's mom, Mavis, answered the door and I heard her quietly say "Um…okay, sure, come in, hold on." Then, she knocked on my bedroom door and said,

"Jessi, the police are here."

NOTES

1. Alexandra Meeks, "With a worsening pandemic, California bans singing in places of worship" CNN.com, July 3, 2020, https://edition.cnn.com/2020/07/03/us/california-places-of-worship-pandemiic-trnd/index.html.

2. Hillary Davis, "In Huntington Beach, a revival with church at the ocean's edge," LATimes.com, July 11, 2020, https://www.latimes.com/socal/daily-pilot/news/story/2020-07-11/in-huntington-beach-a-revival-with-church-at-the-oceans-edge.

CHAPTER 12

Persuasion

The New Testament Church was identified with persecutions,
prisons, and poverty; today many of us are identified with
prosperity, popularity, and personalities.
—**Leonard Ravenhill**, Revival God's Way

W hen I found out the police were at our home, I quickly ran
into our bathroom and whispered loudly, "Parker, Parker,
get out of the shower. The police are here!" Parker quickly
dried off, got dressed, and made his way into our bedroom. With shaking hands I gave Summer over to Mavis and greeted the police officer
and sergeant, both wearing face mask coverings.

I led them to our backyard, and we sat on our outdoor furniture away
from the kids. If we were going to be arrested, I wanted to guard the kids
from the trauma of watching their parents being handcuffed. As I closed
the glass sliding door, I thought to myself, *How far am I willing to go with*
this? What will happen with my kids? If I am in jail, I won't be able to nurse
my newborn baby!

As the police officer and sergeant explained to us the situation, we
went back and forth about the event coming up in two hours. They explained the pressure they were getting from the governor's office. They

felt like they had their hands tied because if they did not shut this down, he threatened to shut down all of Huntington Beach. They reluctantly explained the risks of our gatherings, that we were assembling illegally without a permit, and although the week prior we were given a permit, we were now being refused one without any hope of one in the future. We asked them if they had any suggestions of where people could worship, as we were being told that we could not gather indoors because of "COVID restrictions," but then at the same time we were also being told we can't meet outdoors on a public beach because of COVID and permits. I asked them, "Where can we go worship God and preach the Gospel?"

They had no answer.

The conversation went in circles.

Eventually, the officer wrote us a citation and said that they would be at the beach that evening, and that if we showed up, we risked being arrested. They asked if we understood.

We did.

I had a pink floral dress on for the evening but quickly changed into a T-shirt, long shorts, boots, and a jacket in case I was going to spend the night in jail. Parker's parents agreed to watch our kids if anything happened and picked up formula for the baby. My fingers trembled as tears streamed down my face as I closed the door and said good-bye to my kids.

GO, SHAKING

My friend Tracy picked me up and we stopped to grab a coffee at my favorite coffee shop, Daydream, on the way. As I was waiting for my iced oat milk latte, Parker sent me photos of traffic signs lining the Pacific Coast Highway. The temporary road signs went from Newport to Huntington and culminated at 20th Street outside the beach where we had our planned revival event. "Saturate OC is Cancelled," the signs repeatedly shouted in neon orange to every car that passed by.

I got back into Tracy's car and began to pray in tongues. I opened up my Bible and knew I had to preach a different message tonight. I needed to wake up the Church. I needed to show people that if we don't share the Gospel and change culture, this will be normal.

I looked over at Tracy and said, "Please pray for me, that if it gets crazy, the Spirit will speak through me."

We arrived at the beach, and over a thousand people were there. We told the worship team to go into the middle of the crowd, and we created a circle around them with our team nearby. There was no stage or speakers. We were all together, in a giant circle, right there on the beach.

About eight police vehicles lined the beach near Tower 20. Everyone stood and worshiped and it seemed as though everything was fine. As we continued worshiping, expectancy and passion rose. I saw the police officers come closer in and drive their trucks onto the beach. The spiritual environment was intense to say the least.

Immediately, I saw a vision from when I lived in New York City and the "Occupy Wall Street" protests were happening outside my door. As the police would try to drag away the protestors, they would drop to their knees, making it more difficult to carry them out.

Now, back on the beach, I grabbed the megaphone while shaking and told everyone to "take a knee, that we worship only God, the one true King!"

The intensity increased and worship got louder. Everyone worshiping was risking arrest. This was a holy moment.

Then one of the police officers yelled into a megaphone, "You must leave. This is an illegal assembly."

Everyone went silent, and I began to pray in tongues. The worship leader Tommy looked at me. I just paused. Then a woman in the crowd yelled out, "*Sing louder!*" Her voice carried for what felt like a thousand miles. Everyone *roared* in agreement and we worshiped as if it were the very last breath of praise that would leave our lips. As Tim grabbed a megaphone and began screaming out the song "Tremble," everyone shouted in agreement "Jesus, Jesus, You silence fear!"

I stood up, shaking violently, and looked out at the crowd, at the remnant who were immoveable.

I opened up my Bible and screamed Luke 12:4-12 into the megaphone:

> *I tell you, my friends, do not be afraid of those who kill the body and after that can do no more. But I will show you whom you should fear: Fear him who, after your body has been killed, has authority to throw you into hell. Yes, I tell you, fear him. Are not five sparrows sold for two pennies? Yet not one of them is forgotten by God. Indeed, the very hairs of your head are all numbered. Don't be afraid; you are worth more than many sparrows.*
>
> *I tell you, whoever publicly acknowledges me before others, the Son of Man will also acknowledge before the angels of God. But whoever disowns me before others will be disowned before the angels of God. And everyone who speaks a word against the Son of Man will be forgiven, but anyone who blasphemes against the Holy Spirit will not be forgiven.*
>
> *When you are brought before synagogues, rulers and authorities, do not worry about how you will defend yourselves or what*

*you will say, for the Holy Spirit will teach you at that time what
you should say.*

In a moment, these verses that we had heard in our church pews, with
pretty graphics and flashing lights, all of a sudden had a *very* different
meaning. Jesus Himself was telling us, "When what you are doing is illegal, don't worry about how you will defend yourself—the Holy Spirit
will teach you." Everything I had learned in church culture was being
confronted. I could not believe that these verses did not just pertain to
closed countries—this was now becoming a reality in America!

As I read these words, the crowds roared.

I shared that the price of following Jesus may be a night in jail; the
price one day may be our lives! These are crazy times in our nation; the
times have changed! In my pocket, I had a citation for gathering to worship on the beach. I preached the Gospel and charged everyone to *go* and
saturate their city with the Good News! We needed to take this fire and
spread it in every city this weekend.

Hundreds of people made decisions to follow Jesus and ran into the
water to be baptized.

They prayed and prophesied over the police officers.

The Church was getting her backbone.

We worshiped late into the midnight hour, cold, soaking wet, and full
of fire.

Yes, this, this is revival!

NOW WHAT?

Our email inboxes flooded with requests to bring Saturate to other cities, host more gatherings, baptize more people! Tensions grew on the team, local churches criticized us and posted passive aggressive social media posts about how we were in "rebellion," our car broke down and became un-drivable, they found pipe issues in our house and needed to gut our entire kitchen, and our family (including our new three-month-old baby) was relocated into hotel rooms for eight weeks. All rhythms, routines, and order were disrupted.

Yet we pressed on. Enthralled by what the Lord was doing, absolutely drunk in His Spirit, and living in a real-life dream.

What was originally planned to be four weeks turned into six, moving down the coast to Newport Beach and then to Pirate's Cove in Corona Del Mar. Press inquiries and news reporters came flooding in as we made plans to bring Saturate to San Diego and Santa Cruz.

Over the course of only six weeks in Orange County, thousands had gathered and heard the Gospel, repented, were saved, set free, and baptized.

The crowds demanded more.

After Pirates Cove, I felt like I heard the Lord say to "pause." The crowds began to transition from an army to an audience watching a show. The spiritual atmosphere was shifting again, back into a consumer mindset. Despite the momentum, God was showing me other cities to ignite with the fire of the Gospel.

As September approached, miscommunication on our team began to increase as we made plans to go on the road. There were challenges around where we should go and minister, what our gatherings should look like, and who should lead what areas. My soul became tired. I kept asking God, "What made Saturate work this summer?" and "What is Saturate supposed to be now?!" It felt like we had lost that "togetherness" in lieu of our own individual visions, callings, and ministries.

A pastor who is still a dear friend called me and said, "I just want you to know that we love you and support you. We love Saturate and love everything that God is doing. However, we have our own vision for our city and things that our church is called to do." It was in that moment that I knew this season of Saturate, and how it had looked on the beach, was going to change.

Over the few weeks that followed, I pleaded and asked the Lord, "What can unite people in a city besides a pandemic?"

He responded quietly and patiently, "Passionate prayer by people who are willing to lay it all down over and over again."

Before I could rally another person, or organize another event, I needed to ask myself, "Is that me? Could I lay down Saturate if the Lord asked me to?" I laid on the floor of our prayer room and I said to God, "Here, Lord. I give this to You."

After a few hours, I felt a deep assurance in my soul that the answer was "Yes." I could lay down Saturate if the season was over. I had peace. I deeply want to do whatever the Lord was doing. I wanted the Lord more than I wanted revival.

I think a question we need to continue to ask God is, "What are *You* doing, Lord, and how can I partner with *You*?"

PARTNERING WITH HIS PLANS

My son David has recently been saying something new to me. When he whispers something to me and I don't respond, he says, "Mama, you need to say 'What?'" As I nursed Summer in our prayer room, which has now morphed into her quasi nursery as we begin sleep training, I keep thinking about the importance of that statement. When the Lord is telling us something, most often as a whisper, we need to pause what we are doing, stop the chaos of our busy lives, and say, "What, Lord?" I have found recently that the best question I can be asking God as I learn to steward revival is, "Lord, what are *You* doing? Where is *Your* focus? How can I partner with what *You* want fulfilled?"

I asked the Lord to search me, to keep my heart tender, to help me forgive those who had hurt me in any way. I asked Him to strip from me the bait of the idol of celebrity ministry. A few moments later, I texted Kendra and my mother-in-law Mavis and asked if they would lead a prayer gathering weekly in my house. I spoke with Parker and he agreed that we needed to do this, and it needed to be in our home. For the next three months, we gathered weekly to pray and seek the Lord on the next steps as a collective group, opening our home to 30 to 60 strangers each week.

TOGETHER

If I am honest, so many times I lie wide awake with my heart hurting for the Church and burning for something more. I wonder—is there a company of believers who are *all in*, yielded, desperate, and hungry for the *new* thing the Lord wants to do—who will come together for a *shared* mission?

One day during this season, I woke up and heard the Lord say, "Where there is unity, I will command a blessing."

I responded, "I know, God. I've heard this said a million times."

He then said, "Not unity in the way that you think."

The Hebrew word for *unity* is *yachad*. It means "one accord, alike, together."

In America, we live in an independent culture. It's popular to have individual passions, callings, and even independent ministries. We encourage youth to discover what makes them unique and special among their peers. Church leaders gather at massive conferences and share their missions, values, and vision statements with one another. It's a successful meeting if we've had our coffee, sang some songs, networked a bit, and we say trivial things like, "Awesome, yes, praying for you, supporting you!"

However, I think God is looking for something more.

Revival *requires* something more.

In Acts 4, we see an interesting thing happen among the new believers. Here it says, "They had everything in common." For a moment, in the beginning of Acts, a variety of people were so aware and awakened to the depth, holiness, and Lordship of God because they received the Holy Spirit that they desired nothing else beyond His will.

I believe that summer 2020 we got a taste of what that "togetherness" would feel like, but I believe there is so much more available to us. I pressed in and prayed, "Lord, what is holding us back?"

July 23rd 2020

Waves / Tsunamis / Wildfire / fires up coast
Nehamiah / Deborah

Tonight Parker and I checked into l'Asea hotel —
needing time alone + a place of peace to seek God
and pray and have a clean space.

I truly sense God is moving and I can feel all
thats happening. There is so much in the air—
competition / Apathy / fear. I feel the weight of so
many people offended and unsure what to do and how
to proceed. Lord, I need wisdom!

God, help me to forgive those that persecute me.
Parker spoke to city council and they want us to cancel
tomorrow. The fire dept / police / city attorney want
to shut it down.

God, I believe we are taking ground / taking territory!
Jesus — show me what youre doing, how youre moving.
Fill me with your love / fill me with your Spirit!
Theresa + Levia Dedman gave us words today that
filled us with faith, hope + promises!

Lord — show me what to do! Keep pressing!

!If not Now, then when? !✱

People are dying — they need the Gospel!

So many of us are talking on behalf of _imaginary people_!

Saturate OC

Reverse Alter call

Raise your hand if you are a Christian?

Tonight — many ppl are going to be saved
        many church attendees are going to follow Jesus

After baptism → commission you to _Go_ in groups

Worship + receive the Holy Spirit / get free then _go_!

Every idol being revealed in this _season_.
- mask — offended on / offended off
- gathering — offended do / offended if we dont
- Holy Spirit — too much freedom / not enough
- Religion — hate the speakers / cant hear

Where is Jesus in all of this?

Is Jesus the King or are you?

        Is the goverment
        Are strangers on clg?

Alter Call meet me

(Dont lay hands on me! {Are you not entertained?}

Meet me @ _____
    #Saturate OC   July 31st

! Share the Gospel
Baptize them
Disciple them
Contact US!

Saturate OC

— 167 —

CHAPTER 13

The Secret

Deep in my bones I can feel you
Take me back to a time only we knew
Hideaway...
Say you'll never let me go.
—The Chainsmokers, *"Roses"*

I can probably summarize the heart of this entire book and a major key to revival in Jeremiah 29:12-14 where God says:

> *"Then you will call on me and come and pray to me, and I will listen to you. **You will seek me and find me when you seek me with all your heart.** I will be found by you," declares the Lord, "and will bring you back from captivity. I will gather you from all the nations and places where I have banished you," declares the Lord, "and will bring you back to the place from which I carried you into exile."*

There are so many actionable things from God we can follow from those verses that are so clearly laid out for us:

1. Call on Me.

2. Come.

3. Pray to Me.

4. Seek Me with all your heart.

There are also promises from God when we do those things. He says:

1. I will listen to you.

2. I will be found by you.

3. I will bring you back from captivity.

4. I will gather you (and restore you).

Okay, to paraphrase. If you call out to God and simply say, "Hey, Jesus, I'm here. I want to know *You* more; I am here, and I am listening. What are You doing, Lord?" If you set aside time to be with Him, not to get something out of Him but to simply *be* with Him. If you pray to Him (don't know where to start? Try the Lord's Prayer in Matthew 6:9-13) and truly seek Him, you won't be left empty handed.

The Lord of the universe, the One who created the stars and holds them in His hands, says that *He will listen to you*. That you can actually find God.

I want to dive a little bit into that word *seek*. In Hebrew, it is the word *baqash*. The word has an abundance of definitions. The Lord is saying, "When you search out (by any method, specifically in worship or prayer); strive after, beg, beseech, desire, enquire, get, make inquisition, procure, require Me with your whole heart—I promise to be found by you." The Lord wants our passion; He wants our heart. He doesn't want to be an option.

One of my favorite books this fall! *Why Revival Tarries* by Leonard Ravenhill who is a SAVAGE!

PRAYER GRASPS ETERNITY

Ravenhill - strikes
Again!

NO man is greater than his prayer life. The pastor who is not praying is playing; the people who are not praying are straying. The pulpit can be a shop-window to display one's talents; the prayer closet allows no showing off.

Poverty-stricken as the Church is today in many things, she is most stricken here, in the place of prayer. We have many organizers, but few agonizers; many players and payers, few pray-ers; many singers, few clingers; lots of pastors, few wrestlers; many fears, few tears; much fashion, little passion; many interferers, few intercessors; many writers, but few fighters. Failing here, we fail everywhere.

The two prerequisites to successful Christian living are vision and passion, both of which are born in and maintained by prayer. The ministry of preaching is open to few; the ministry of prayer—the highest ministry of all human offices—is open to all. Spiritual adolescents say, "I'll not go tonight, it's only the prayer meeting." It may be that Satan has little cause to fear

THE SECRET TO REVIVAL IS THE SECRET PLACE

Nothing has shaped me more than learning to "dwell in the shelter of the Most High" (see Ps. 91:1). Leading Saturate has been an emotional roller coaster. Yet each criticism, each blow, each disappointment didn't sting as much as many expected. When the fiery arrows of accusation came my way, I knew where I could hide. The last ten years have really prepared me through tiny trials and disappointments to run into the secret place. The Lord promises to listen to you if you will call on Him. Lord Jesus, thank You. Thank You! Thank You for giving us access to You!

God is so incredibly amazing; I wish I had the words to express it. All I can do is live a life that shows my gratitude to Him. Not only does God listen to us and reveal Himself to us, He even says, "I will bring you back from captivity" (see Jer. 29:14). This means He will restore your fortunes, *what was promised to you*. Figuratively, a former state of prosperity. Everything that was stolen from you, the Lord will return to you! I want to throw my computer down, run down the street, and preach this as loud as I can! This means that as you spend time in His presence, He restores you to be the person you were created to be and brings back to you (with interest!) what the enemy has stolen!

THE SECRET PLACE PRODUCES LIFE

You, Lord, are my lamp; the Lord turns my darkness into light (2 Samuel 22:29).

The New Age movement is growing increasingly popular, especially in California. I am surprised by how many Christians have adopted "new age" philosophy. When I was deep in depression, a friend gave me a New Age book called *The Secret*. I read the book and the "big" secret is essentially positive thinking and the law of attraction. I practiced what the book said because I was not following Jesus and was searching for answers. I knew there was more to life than I was experiencing. As I made my vision boards, visualized my dream job, expensive shoes that I wanted, and vacations I wanted to go on, something interesting happened. *It worked.*

I know that isn't what you were expecting me to write.

However, you don't sell millions of copies of a book on "positive thinking" if it doesn't actually work, right? I had "manifested" the $1,300 shoes I wanted, the promotion at work, traveled first class around the world, and more. What the book failed to mention (there should be a warning label on those New Age books!) is that *there was a cost*. You see, I had made myself into my own little god. I had become the god of my own tiny universe. I was not dreaming with God, repenting of my sins, and seeking His ways. Oh no, quite the contrary. So with my fancy shoes came demons as well—the little gift wrap on your "gift from the universe." Depression increased, and with it came anxiety and suicidal thoughts—the feeling of "always wanting," yet never satisfied.

I was unaware of Galatians at the time, but since following Jesus I can read these Scriptures and see so clearly how so many are being taken out by the enemy. Horoscopes, crystals, witchcraft, psychics, "*the universe*," "*manifesting your dreams*," and other New Age philosophies may "work" temporarily but will ultimately lead to destruction. Oftentimes, the Church can look no different. As we preach messages to build up our identities, callings, increase blessings, and grow our ministry, we are all focusing on God serving *us* and not us serving God! Then we wonder why each year we are running to the altars to get deliverance yet never finding true freedom!

There is no *"secret."* God has already given us the keys, full access to *His Kingdom* in *His Word* through *His Spirit.*

In Galatians 5:19-21, it says:

> *It is obvious what kind of life develops out of trying to get your own way all the time: repetitive, loveless, cheap sex; a stinking accumulation of mental and emotional garbage; frenzied and joyless grabs for happiness; trinket gods; magic-show religion; paranoid loneliness; cutthroat competition; all-consuming-yet-never-satisfied wants; a brutal temper; an impotence to love or be loved; divided homes and divided lives; small-minded and lopsided pursuits; the vicious habit of depersonalizing everyone into a rival; uncontrolled and uncontrollable addictions; ugly parodies of community. I could go on. This isn't the first time I have warned you, you know. If you use your freedom this way, you will not inherit God's kingdom (MSG).*

If you were reading those words and any of that felt familiar or "too real," this may be an opportunity to get into *the secret place,* ask Jesus to forgive you, ask Him to heal your heart and your mind and fill you with His Holy Spirit. I believe that many of you reading this right now are thinking, *Well, my life doesn't look like all of those things…just a few.*

Here is the reality. Jesus didn't die on the cross for your sins and rise from the dead to leave you half free. Don't settle and allow the enemy to rob you of the full free life that God has for you. There is a stark difference between life in the Spirit and life in the flesh. You should be able to tell the difference!

Galatians 5:22-26 goes on:

*But what happens when we live God's way? He brings gifts into
our lives, much the same way that fruit appears in an orchard—
things like affection for others, exuberance about life, serenity.
We develop a willingness to stick with things, a sense of compassion in the heart, and a conviction that a basic holiness per-
meates things and people. We find ourselves involved in loyal
commitments, not needing to force our way in life, able to marshal and direct our energies wisely.*

*Legalism is helpless in bringing this about; it only gets in the
way. Among those who belong to Christ, everything connected
with getting our own way and mindlessly responding to what
everyone else calls necessities is killed off for good—crucified.*

*Since this is the kind of life we have chosen, the life of the Spirit,
let us make sure that we do not just hold it as an idea in our
heads or a sentiment in our hearts, but work out its implications
in every detail of our lives. That means we will not compare
ourselves with each other as if one of us were better and another
worse. We have far more interesting things to do with our lives.
Each of us is an original* (MSG).

OPEN RELATIONSHIP

Months after I was saved in my bedroom, I got back together with
Drew. (I know what you're thinking, but we are all like dogs returning to

vomit when we are living in the flesh!) Our relationship was constantly on again, off again. We were in this limbo of a relationship, and it was driving me a bit crazy. One evening, we were sitting on the couch and he said to me, "So Jessi, obviously this has been really messy." I shook my head "yes" in agreement, my heart heavy, and my hands clammy. He said, "You know, I think I have an idea. I think we should be in an open relationship."

I paused for a moment and hesitantly asked, "What's that?"

He confidently responded, "Well, it's this really great thing. So, when we're together, it's like we are dating. We'll go out to dinner, have fun adventures, go to all these cool places. We'll be in an exclusive relationship when we're together. But when we're not together, you can see other people and I can see other people. Don't worry though, when we were together, we won't talk about that."

I know it sounds absolutely crazy, and for those who know me now, they would hardly believe it, but the sad part of this story is I agreed to these terms! I said to him that night, "Okay, I guess that sounds reasonable." I remember leaving that night feeling so broken. I cried the entire cab ride home.

I stayed in that "open relationship" for two months. The pain of being without him was almost unbearable. I thought having a little bit of a relationship was better than having nothing at all. I was just beginning my journey of following Jesus and didn't know any other Christians besides my parents. I had one foot in the world, and one foot in the Kingdom. When you feel hopeless, you don't know what the right decision is. You're just desperate.

Years later, as I was happily married to Parker, I woke up on a random Thursday morning remembering the scenario with Drew. My heart hurt; it felt like a thousand kettlebells were placed on my chest remembering this conversation. I ran out to Parker in the living room and begged for him to pray for me. After we prayed, I went back into our bedroom and I read the Bible. As I was reading, God said to me, "Jessi, it's going to be okay. I love you. I understand how you felt. Do you know, there are so many people who come to church every Sunday and they're in an open relationship with Me?"

I started weeping into my pillow. I could feel in my spirit the anguish the Lord felt, even if it was just a glimmer. He continued, "They come to church on Sunday, and when they're with Me, they're with Me! They're raising their hands in worship and they're praising Me. However, when Monday comes, they do whatever they want, they don't talk about it with Me. Each day, they go about their lives and do whatever they desire, and they live completely separate from Me."

I said, "Jesus, why don't You yell at them? Why do You even allow that? You're God! I was not God in that relationship, obviously, but You, You're God."

You know what He said to me? He said, "I'm desperate for them. *I'm desperate for them*! I love them so much that even when they give me no relationship in return, I still died on the cross for them. So, when they give me a little bit, I'll take it 'cause I can work with a little bit, *but I want all of them*. The greatest thing about a relationship is commitment because there's trust, and where there's trust, there is promise. When there is commitment, there are no more secrets; they get full access."

CHAPTER 14

Burn

C. S. Lewis writes, our faith is not a matter of our hearing what Christ said long ago and "trying to carry it out." Rather, "The real Son of God is at your side. He is beginning to turn you into the same kind of thing as Himself. He is beginning, so to speak, to 'inject' His kind of life and thought, His Zoe [life], into you; beginning to turn the tin soldier into a live man. The part of you that does not like it is the part that is still tin."
—**Dallas Willard,** The Divine Conspiracy

I believe that all along God is preparing us for the very things *He* has in store for us. When we moved to California to start Salt Churches in 2016, Parker and I were in a bit of a "wrecking" season. I call it our "threshing floor" year! Recently, Parker pointed out to me that the threshing floor can be the very place for the fire on the altar to burn (see 1 Chron. 21:22-30). I believe that during that year, God was taking us through a series of tests and lessons to strengthen and refine our hearts and character to withstand the many things He was calling us into so that we could *burn* with His presence.

So often we can get caught up in the idea of the next "big thing." We want revival, but we don't want to be the kind of people who *steward* revival. We want the excitement, the miracles, the big crowds, and the favor without the long nights of preparation, the sacrifice, the tears, the rejection, and the resilience to *obey* against all odds. Retrospect is a beautiful thing. Looking back, I can see a few ways that the Lord was taking us through some trials that have prepared us for what we are now leading in California and beyond.

LESSONS OF FIRE-MAKING ONE: TINDER / FAITH

Jesus said to him, "If you can believe, all things are possible to him who believes" (Mark 9:23 NKJV).

Sometimes, I read this verse and I think, *really? Could this really be true? All things?* Some of the dreams that God has deposited into me seem *so* impossible.

In faith, we need to *not accept reality for what it is.* This is the territory where we need to press in for deeper revelation. We need to grow in belief. Without faith, we absolutely cannot fulfill the things God is calling us into. If prayer is the seed for revival, faith is the soil. We need to not just pray weak, lifeless prayers! We need to pray with faith! We need to *see* what God is doing and call it down to earth.

How to *increase your faith:*

1. First, you need to receive the gift of faith, which is given to every single person. Ephesians 2:8 says, "For it is by grace

you have been saved, through faith—and this is not from yourselves, it is the gift of God."

2. Faith comes from hearing. Romans 10:17 says, "Consequently, faith comes from hearing the message, and the message is heard through the word about Christ."

3. Faith comes from *doing* the *Word*. James 1:22 says, "But don't just listen to God's word. You must do what it says. Otherwise, you are only fooling yourselves" (NLT).

4. Faith comes from trials and difficulty. James 1:2-3 says, "Count it all joy, my brothers, when you meet trials of various kinds, for you know that the testing of your faith produces steadfastness" (ESV).

The truth is, the Kingdom of God is much more *real* than the very chair you are sitting in. Daily, we need to deny ourselves and receive more faith. As we obey God in our tiny daily "Yeses," we begin to transform our mind and reality. The world is constantly trying to convince us that the things we see with our natural eyes are "more real." We need to know the Word of God by praying and reading Scripture.

If God created the heavens and the earth—all reality is subject to Him. Our faith is a greater reality than what we see. If He created it, can't He do anything?

LESSONS OF FIRE-MAKING TWO: FUEL / THE SPIRIT

When the Holy Spirit came upon those first believers at Pentecost, they suddenly had all the power they needed to follow Christ, even to the death, if needed. Even the disciples who walked with Jesus in the flesh fell short in their own strength. While Jesus was on earth, He promised the Spirit.

> *But the Advocate, the Holy Spirit, whom the Father will send in my name, will teach you all things and will remind you of everything I have said to you (John 14:26).*

Through the power of the Holy Spirit, we can become transformed from the inside out. After being baptized in the Holy Spirit, Peter preached with power:

> *Peter's words pierced their hearts, and they said to him and to the other apostles, "Brothers, what should we do?" Peter replied, "Each of you must repent of your sins and turn to God, and be baptized in the name of Jesus Christ for the forgiveness of your sins. Then you will receive the gift of the Holy Spirit. This promise is to you, to your children, and to those far away—all who have been called by the Lord our God" (Acts 2:37-39 NLT).*

The same Peter who denied Jesus now spoke with boldness and led thousands into repentance and salvation through Jesus. It is impossible to be Spirit-filled and live apathetically. There is an overflow that will come as you allow the Holy Spirit to consume you. Your "dry season" is over. Jesus says that you shall live in *overflow*:

> *In the last day, that great day of the feast, Jesus stood and cried, saying, If any man thirst, let him come unto me, and drink. He*

that believeth on me, as the scripture hath said, out of his belly shall flow rivers of living water. (But this spake he of the Spirit, which they that believe on him should receive: for the Holy Ghost was not yet given; because that Jesus was not yet glorified) (John 7:37-39 KJV).

This is the life God has for you, a life of overflow. God wants to fill you with His Holy Spirit to spark wildfires everywhere you go!

The wildfires we recently had in California were unstoppable because of all the dead wood that the flames consumed. If we learn to welcome the Holy Spirit into our own hearts to burn away anything that is bringing death, we ourselves can be ignited to burn with His passion and bring an unstoppable Kingdom.

LESSONS OF FIRE-MAKING THREE: SPARK / SUBMISSION

Will we bow to culture, fear of man, politics, popularity, ambition, and the wisdom of the world?

This is a lesson that I believe God is constantly taking us all through. It is impossible to read the Bible and not see the war between submission to culture and submission to God. Some of the heart lessons we have learned from previous seasons of pioneering and stepping out in faith include a refining of our hearts in the following areas. Could we:

+ Lay down our platforms?

+ Release control and let go of our way of doing things?

- Trust God when it came to finances?

- Steward a new idea?

- Turn down opportunities that "look good"?

- Pioneer when no one understands?

- Prioritize His presence over everything?

So often, we either get distracted, choose comfort, or are honestly just kind of flakey when it comes to commitments, keeping our word, and obeying God.

I shared recently on social media, "Being flakey isn't a spiritual gift." Many people commented and laughed, because it's true. We make plans, we break them. We "commit to one another" then don't show up, all under the guise of being Spirit led. If your Spirit-led life is constantly leaving others high and dry, it may be a good time to ask, "What spirit is leading me?"

I have noticed one defining factor to why some people actually get to be a part of leading great moves of God through revival history while others seem to let it pass them by. Want to know the "big secret"?

You have to show up.

I know, it's pretty crazy. You literally don't even need any theological training to simply show up.

In our micro churches, we have a young leader named Victoria. Victoria is someone I constantly want to promote. I look for ways to promote her because she does the simple and annoying tasks without complaint and without overly complicating things. She does what needs to be done without overly spiritualizing every tiny task. She doesn't need to tell me that she is "for me" because I know through her actions that she is. When I need her, she shows up. Simply put. Are we with Him and His plans through merely good intentions, or do our calendars actually reflect that we are prioritizing the things that are important to God? Go and check!

In 2020, we were all slammed with many controversial and life altering issues. I look around and see many churches' social media feeds looking exactly like the mainstream media and a pagan society. Culture and media are demanding a response from the Church. And we are bowing our heads and hearts, quickly joining in on every political and social bandwagon that masquerades as compassion without the Gospel message of reconciliation to God the Father through Christ Jesus. Where is the higher perspective? Is anyone out there saying, "Hold up…maybe I don't need to respond right away. Heck! Maybe I should even turn my phone off for a few weeks and pray, ask God what He thinks about all of this"?

Could you imagine?!

Okay, I am obviously being a bit sarcastic, because there are so many people who do that, but come on, friends! We got to get better at not just jumping on whatever social media justice bandwagon comes into town. We are *the Church!* We should be hearing from Heaven and bringing Heaven's solutions.

Are we submitted to God's plans over our own agendas? Has our desire to keep people in our Sunday services and keep people happy prevented our ability to bring the Kingdom? How has hope become so controversial? I shared online that I believed that God was going to move powerfully in 2020, despite what we were seeing on the news. Hundreds of people unfollowed me. They commented that I was "missing the point and not addressing the issues."

Let me write this so it's crystal clear.

The Church should *always be* front and center in addressing issues.

The first and foremost issue is that there *is no* hope, freedom, or reconciliation outside of Christ. For those of you who are ministers, I'd even dare say that you almost have *no right* to address any other issue until your church is a soul-winning church! Once your congregation has gotten their priorities straight—that souls are perishing for all of eternity and they have the solution, that Jesus is alive and we serve a resurrected King, that the Holy Spirit is the third Person of the Trinity and we must repent for ignoring Him and quenching Him from our services—*then* we can do a sermon series on how to manage a budget, on racial reconciliation, or on building a great community.

We as the American Church don't believe that we have idols. The truth is, we are just better at hiding them. Evangelist Chris Overstreet wrote in *A Practical Guide to Evangelism*, "If we are willing to regularly submit ourselves to the leading of the Holy Spirit, and will choose to live a lifestyle of risk, we will be the supernatural answer that the world is waiting for."

LESSONS OF FIRE-MAKING FOUR: SUSTAIN / DISCIPLESHIP

When we started Salt Churches, we had no paradigm for how to multiply churches that would stay on mission to make disciples who would then multiply. Parker kept asking the following three questions when we were envisioning what a micro church would be like:

1. How do we help people have unbroken fellowship with Jesus?

2. How do we simplify so that anyone can be empowered to start a church?

3. How do we make disciples who make disciples who know how to share the Gospel, live in freedom, and are filled with the Holy Spirit?

Six months into starting Salt Churches, I hosted a women's event called "Lux Night." It was an awesome and beautiful event at a trendy coffee shop in Newport. I rented out the space, ordered lattes and pastries for every woman, and 50 women bought tickets to attend!

The next week, Parker killed Lux Night.

It wasn't because he hates women's events (well, he kinda does, ha ha, shhh!), but it was because I couldn't answer the question he asked me, which was, "How does Lux Night reach the lost and make disciples?"

Someone once asked us, "Do you think house churches are biblical?"

Someone else asked, "Why start something new? You are great at leading legacy churches, don't waste your gifting."

Yet Parker couldn't shake this idea that maybe we had complicated things. He couldn't do anything else but try to simplify with God. This unfamiliar territory created the uncomfortable space we needed as leaders to pioneer with God, to birth Saturate, and to do many of the things we are doing now when it comes to "ministry."

Sometimes you have to kill what's familiar to do what is new.

This unfamiliar territory created the uncomfort-  able space we needed as leaders to pioneer with God, to birth Saturate, and do many of the things we are doing now when it comes to "ministry."

In 2015, I was facing a difficult reality. There was a big difference between what Jesus promises in the Bible and what my life actually looked like. John 14:12 would ring in my ear on the subway, at work, while falling asleep: "Very truly I tell you, whoever believes in me will do the works I have been doing, and they will do even greater things than these, because I am going to the Father."

Let's break this down.

If you believe in Jesus—you will do what Jesus does.

You will do greater things.

While speaking at a conference in Georgia, this guy named Clint who was one of the leaders of Adventures in Mission (who is close to an exact replica of Ed Norton in *Fight Club*, both in looks and charisma) reached out to my husband and me. He simply said, "Come follow me, and I'll make you fishers of men." I sat in silence. Was he allowed to say that? Can you steal Jesus' lines and make them your own? I was intrigued.

We set up a Skype call (mostly out of curiosity), and we talked about discipleship. We talked about following Jesus. Not who we thought Jesus was, but who Jesus actually *is*. Our only requirement was to give away whatever we received. The Bible says to do that 100 times or more, so I was okay with the terms.

After two weeks, I started meeting bi-weekly with two other women, mainly just processing what Clint was processing with my husband and me. Their only requirement was to give away whatever they received.

The Bible says in Matthew 28:19:

> *Therefore go and make disciples of all nations, baptizing them*
> *in the name of the Father and of the Son and of the Holy Spirit.*

I could not believe that in all of my "ministry efforts" I had so easily neglected the Great Commission. The Bible does not tell us to associate ourselves as Christians, to just attend church, or to have good morals. We are called to become followers of Jesus and to lead other people to become followers as well.

Setting aside time to meet intentionally with the people you disciple, studying the Word, and then practicing *obeying* what it says is radical! God's Word is living and transforms us, if we will yield to the knife.

The first resistance I hear from people when we start talking about the concept of discipleship is that they don't feel "qualified" to disciple anyone, or they are not being discipled themselves, or that they don't have enough time. If you read your Bible and love Jesus, just find two people to meet with bi-weekly and process with them what you're reading in Scripture. Ask them, "What is Jesus saying to you when you read this?" When I meet with my disciples, the conversation often starts with, "What has God been showing you lately?" and "How is it going with your disciples?"—then I see how the Holy Spirit moves from there.

What if discipleship means waking up at 7 a.m. to get coffee twice a month with two people and reading the Bible together, and then they meet with two people, who meet with two people, and so on? Could it be that simple? Could this revival be sustained by the saints sacrificing four hours a month of their very important schedules?

I honestly believe with every fiber of my being that discipleship is the key to sustained revival. I don't think Jesus was kidding when He said, "Go and make disciples." We are coming up with all of these strategies to reach the lost, build our churches, and see a movement of God.

What if *we* are the movement of God?

PART 4

Traps

Elijah lived with God. He thought about the nation's sin like God; he grieved over sin like God; he spoke against sin like God. He was all passion in his prayers and passionate in his denunciation of evil in the land. He had no smooth preaching. Passion fired his preaching, and his words were on the hearts of men as molten metal on their flesh.

—Leonard Ravenhill, *Why Revival Tarries*

CHAPTER 15

Revolt Against Apathy

It's better to feel pain than nothing at all
The opposite of love's indifference
So pay attention now.
I'm standing on your porch screaming out
And I won't leave until you come downstairs.
So keep your head up, keep your love.
—Lumineers, "Stubborn Love"

ap·a·thy /ˈapəTHē/ (noun)

1. lack of interest, enthusiasm, or concern.

2. behavior that shows no interest or energy and shows that someone is unwilling to take action, especially over something important.[1]

I wonder if there is anything worse than the plague of apathy. We were never meant to live apathetically. We were made in the image of God, whether we believe in Him or not. We were designed to feel. Our Creator designed us with senses to touch, feel, taste, see, hear, and respond to the world around us.

Did you know that the word *passion* was originated to describe Jesus going to the cross?

The English word has its roots in the Latin *passio*, which means "suffering." Its first recorded use is in early Latin translations of the Bible that appeared in the second century A.D. used to describe the death of Jesus.[2]

We throw around the word *passion* so loosely and use it incorrectly all the time. We say things like, "I'm passionate about cooking" or "follow your passions." Passion far exceeds excitement. They had to create this word to describe the suffering of Christ on the cross. What Christ did for you and me, what He endured, was deep, physical suffering out of His desire for us to live free lives and be one with the Father. The word *passion* was created to describe our Savior, our Lord, the One whom we follow and yield our lives to. How then have we become so deceived to believe that our lives should lack interest in the world around us? How have we been muted to the point of waking up, going to work, making a few meals, and then going back to sleep, all to do the same routine over and over again?

Why, why have we become unwilling to take action when what is happening around us is so important to God? How can you spend time in His presence and still lack enthusiasm? How can you watch the news and witness policies being passed that murder children in the birth canal and not act? How can you stand there and only spectate while rioters pillage small business owners' shops and burn down our cities? How can you keep scrolling on your newsfeed as our nation cries out for justice on blood-filled streets while denying the name of Jesus?

This stirs me so deeply that I needed the subtitle of this book to say, "Revolt Against Apathy." As I write this, the presence of God is engulfing my room and tears are streaming down my face. I am fervently typing and working late, long hours with the help of Larry, Tina, and the rest of the Destiny Image team to get this book into your hands as soon as possible. When I wrote this chapter, I was right in the midst of planning a tent revival the following week, and my to-do list was pages long, but that needed to wait because these words needed to be written *for you.*

We need *you* to revolt against apathy. There cannot be a Great *Awakening* while you lack interest and enthusiasm.

REVOLT

I know *revolt* seems like a pretty strong word, but the definition of revolt is:

re·volt | \ ri-'vōlt also -'volt \

1. to renounce allegiance or subjection (as to a government): REBEL

2. to experience disgust or shock

Cambridge Dictionary says:

If a large number of people revolt, they refuse to be controlled or ruled, and take action against authority, often violent action; to take violent action against authority, or to refuse to be controlled or ruled.[3]

What I am encouraging you to do is to refuse to be controlled or ruled by the demonic stronghold of apathy. We need to get violent!

Matthew 11:12 says, "From the days of John the Baptist until now the kingdom of heaven suffers violent assault, and violent men seize it by force [as a precious prize]" (AMP).

The Kingdom is our precious prize—stop allowing yourself to be pillaged. There's a term in the art and film industry called *visual lethargy*. This term means that we can see something over and over again and become desensitized to it. We have probably all experienced this watching mainstream news. One report after another—how can we even begin to care anymore? We become empathetically exhausted. We have to snuff out our spirit so we can get breakfast made, get our kids dressed for school, and not lay in bed in a puddle of tears while the earth is groaning.

So how do we revolt against apathy as it lulls us to sleep while our house is burning to the ground?

PAY ATTENTION

G.K. Chesterton wrote, "There is no such thing on earth as an uninteresting subject; the only thing that can exist is an uninterested person."[4]

It's time to stop for a moment and look at your life. Have you grown apathetic? Your calling is usually tied to the things that you are passionate about. This means you are willing to endure suffering to see them come to pass. Revival is no easy task and not for the faint of heart, trust me. I have wanted to quit 1,893 times this year. Yet my heart has not grown apathetic, even when I have felt alone and cried out to the Lord, asking Him, "God, why does it seem like no one cares? My hand is on the plow and I can't watch one more person post about revival when they don't show up!"

If you have grown apathetic, it is time to realign yourself with the One who creates life.

FOLLOWERS OF THE WAY

In John 14:6-7, Jesus said, "I am the way and the truth and the life. No one comes to the Father except through me. If you really know me, you will know my Father as well. From now on, you *do* know him and have seen him."

The early followers of Jesus were called the "Followers of the Way." They were marked by living a life in full submission to Christ. It was not their Sunday attendance that made them followers; it was their daily *choosing* to follow and a life transformed by surrender.

Sometimes following Jesus can feel hard. When He preached difficult teachings or unpopular sermons that didn't get the *amen* from the crowd, many would often leave. After Jesus preached the famous "eat my flesh and drink my blood" sermon, He said to the disciples:

> *"Do you want to go away as well?" Simon Peter answered him,*
> *"Lord, to whom shall we go? You have the words of eternal life,*
> *and we have believed, and have come to know, that you are the*
> *Holy One of God"* (John 6:67-69 ESV).

Peter chose to follow Jesus because *only* Jesus had the words of eternal life.

Are we following a made-up Jesus? A Jesus who brings us comfort and prosperity as we live out our Christian spin on the American dream? Let's press in, go deeper, and follow the Jesus who gives life!

LIVING BY FAITH

Living by faith has been hard for me.

Honestly.

Since moving to California, there have been several moments when I have opened up applications to apply for marketing jobs because I wanted to "quit" ministry that wasn't working, make six figures, and not have to stress about paying rent each month. We currently live by support, which makes our budget pretty tight. When we were leaving New York, we were in the best financial situation since our marriage. We were both full-time paid staff at church, and my creative agency was exploding, allowing me to make an additional salary, hire staff, and have extra time to do street evangelism.

Sometimes God will ask you to lay down a "good thing" for a "God thing."

The reality is, we haven't had financial stability for the four years since we moved here. When we decided to live by faith and give away my business to a friend in 2018, I said "yes," but I said it hesitantly. My natural mind couldn't understand! Why would I give away my business for free when we needed the money?!

However, in exchange for "providing for myself," we have received *life*. Like real *life* and passion. God needed me to create the mental space and time in my schedule to birth Saturate and multiply disciples through micro churches. Now, we are seeing our wildest, most impossible dreams come true. Our rent has miraculously been paid every month! I'm talking surprise checks in the mail. I know, it sounds so crazy. My faith has grown so much and is still growing.

I keep hearing the Lord say, "My beautiful daughter, you can trust Me. You can really trust Me to provide for you *wherever I lead you*."

I want to encourage you, spend time with God in His presence. Ask Him to lead you into a life of risk. The truth is, God will provide for you wherever *He leads you*. I believe that many of you are called into the marketplace, as I was for eight years. I believe that there are many in ministry being called into media, education, politics, entertainment, and beyond!

DON'T ALLOW YOUR EMOTIONS TO LEAD YOU

I met with a group of former missionaries a few years ago and invited them to come do street ministry with me because the night before, many of them expressed a desire to see God's power move in America.

When it was time to meet at the van to head into town, three people showed up.

When I later asked one of the girls (who was wailing in prayer the night before for revival) why she didn't end up coming, she responded, "I didn't feel led."

Five people got saved that afternoon. One woman's back was healed miraculously.

Want to see revival?

Preach the Gospel, even if you don't feel like it.

Show up when there is an invitation to the thing you have been praying for.

Acts 1:8 says, "But you will receive power when the Holy Spirit comes on you; and you will be my witnesses."

Let's stop posting on social media about God's power with fancy typography and let's start preaching with power! There are already so many talkers; we need some practitioners. If you feel stuck, find some people who are on fire! We need you! America needs you! Jesus has given you all that you need! Can you imagine what God has in store for our collective *yes?!* I don't think we have the capability to think on this scale—*He wants nations!*

NOTES

1. *Cambridge Dictionary*, s.v. "Apathy," https://dictionary.cambridge.org/us/dictionary/english/apathy.

2. Sam Schechner, "Why Is It Called The Passion?" Slate.com, February 24, 2004, https://slate.com/news-and-politics/2004/02/why-is-it-called-the-passion.html.

3. *Cambridge Dictionary*, s.v. "Revolt," https://dictionary.cambridge.org/us/dictionary/english/revolt.

4. G.K. Chesterton, *Heretics*, in *The Three Apologies of G.K. Chesterton: Heretics, Orthodoxy & The Everlasting Man* (Mockingbird Press, 2018), 13.

CHAPTER 16

Lies Are Clues

She has been through hell, so believe me when I say, fear her when she looks into a fire and smiles.

—e. corona

Okay, let's admit it. Spiritual warfare is a real thing that is sometimes messy, scary, and confusing for the average believer. I remember sitting in my bedroom reading *Spirit Wars* by Kris Vallotton and *Deliverance from Evil Spirits* by Francis MacNutt and thinking to myself, *I am definitely not reading this anymore before bedtime. This is scary stuff!*

Like it or not, Hollywood has played a role in our perception of the spiritual realm. In ministry, we often have to use words like "freedom prayer" instead of "deliverance" to encourage people to sign up to have demons cast out of them. I had no idea what we would be stepping into when it came to spiritual warfare. You can read all the books on strategies of warfare and still feel so inadequately prepared when the enemy is raging against you. We have seen thousands of people set free from demonic influences on the beaches through Saturate. So many of the things I have learned have come by "in the field" combat training!

My friend Leah has a theory called "the lies are clues." In this theory, she believes that the ways we are lied to can be a confirmation of what God is doing in the opposite spirit. Since she shared this revelation, I have disciplined myself to write down the ways we are spiritually attacked, the lies I believe, and the times I have wanted to quit or give up or feel "anti-anointed." I then take these notes and bring them into the secret place and ask the Holy Spirit to reveal the truth to me. Usually there is a powerful exchange of truth for lies that takes place.

HOUSE FIRE

In the spring of 2019, not long after we had our initial vision casting dinner for pastors in the region to partner with Saturate, Parker was away at a men's retreat in Montana. I was at home alone with our two toddler boys at the time and was settling in for the night. Victoria and Kendall agreed to come over and spend the night and help me with the kids in the morning. As we sat chatting on the couch, I heard a large *pop!* It sounded a bit like a gunshot. I jumped up and ran into the kitchen where I heard the sound. It didn't seem like anything was out of place. I called Parker and explained what happened and he said to call 911 if I noticed anything suspicious.

A few moments later, the house smelled like burning plastic. Kendall looked in the kitchen and saw flames coming out under our dishwasher. I immediately called the fire department and we woke the children up, grabbed them in our arms and a backpack of a few items, and ran out the front door. The flames began to consume the kitchen as the fire department arrived. There were four firetrucks lining my street, and the brave men ran toward the flames and put the fire out.

It was around 11:30 p.m. as we stood in the cold, holding the kids, just waiting to hear the outcome. Our landlord Karl arrived, and we explained to him what happened. After about a half hour, the firefighters emerged from the smoky house. They explained that we would need to stay in a hotel for the night because of all the smoke.

It honestly was a miracle we all got out okay because the smoke detectors didn't go off. If I hadn't been waiting for Kendall to drive down from L.A. to sleep over, I would have been deep asleep and not have seen the flames. The fear of what could have happened to my children kept racing through my head.

I wrote on my Instagram a few days later:

> The last three days we have been in three different hotel rooms, nap times have been a wreck, and we just found out that we won't be able to be back in the house for 2-3 weeks till they fix the damage. I spoke to so many insurance people, cried about 30 times, and still haven't landed on our temporary housing. This weekend we are hosting a Salt Churches summit, that was set to be in our house. While I'm searching for where we will sleep, we are also now searching for a venue for the weekend. I'm so thankful for the friends that have sent us money to help cover our hotel these last three days, for my Salt family that has watched our dog Nugget and helped with the boys and sent prophetic words to encourage me while I wait for Parker to return from his trip. While I was crying by the pool, I decided to put my phone down (and not keep waiting on insurance) and swim with the boys for an hour. I thanked Jesus that we were safe and tried to make the best of the moment and just stated, this will be a blessing in disguise—I know it!

One night in a hotel turned into seven weeks of being displaced. Although we were displaced for nearly the whole summer of 2019, it truly was a blessing in disguise. We ended up getting an incredible AirBNB in Newport Beach to host the Salt Church Planting Summit, and then were moved to Palm Springs. We turned our "displacement" into a retreat and put our phones on "airplane mode" and took time together to pray and rest! Financially, God provided for us in a myriad of ways.

Now, I am not going to create an entire theology around spiritual "attacks" happening when you lead revival. However, I will say that you can expect that the enemy is going to try to bring in a counter-attack when God is moving.

CURSES

There are so many incredible books and resources on spiritual warfare that you can purchase, so I only want to briefly touch on the subject. I am no expert when it comes to spiritual warfare, and to be honest, in many ways I was blindsided this past summer of 2020. However, I want to encourage you, wherever you may be feeling attacked, there is greater protection.

Anytime we felt the fiery darts coming in our direction, I felt like there was a shield of protection over me. I asked God what it was, and He said it was faith.

> *Having fastened on the belt of truth, and having put on the breastplate of righteousness, and, as shoes for your feet, having put on the readiness given by the gospel of peace. In all circumstances take up the shield of faith, with which you can extinguish*

all the flaming darts of the evil one; and take the helmet of sal-
vation, and the sword of the Spirit, which is the word of God
(Ephesians 6:14-17 ESV).

I believe that shield of faith was beyond my faith; it was also the faith of the many people surrounding us in prayer. I can't begin to tell you how important it is to have yourself surrounded by prayer warriors!

Two years before Saturate, my friend Tami had started a lunch gathering of female revivalists called Revivalist OC. Through this lunch, I had met so many on-fire women who were madly in love with Jesus, running their race, and in my corner. As I stepped into pioneering Saturate, I knew I needed to have people I could go deep with. I reached out to Joanne and Tracy and asked that they would be people I could trust and have "no filter" with them. Meaning, I would "go there" despite my discomfort, be vulnerable, text them when I felt attacked, and would receive open feedback from them if I had any blind spots. I can't tell you how many times I had to text them to "quickly pray" when I felt fear, got sick, or noticed discouragement or hopelessness seep in.

DON'T GLORIFY THE ATTACK

Some of you may not like to hear this, but nevertheless it must be said. Too many times we give satan way too much glory. The first Friday of revival meetings we hosted with Saturate on the beach in 2020, they found black mold in our kitchen. Upon further inspection, they decided they had to gut our entire kitchen, and our house became unlivable once again.

As I was texting the worship team with logistics for the second weekend on the beach, I was trying to find the best rates for a hotel to stay in locally. We checked in, and Parker went away to the woods for a few days to get some peace of mind. Upon his return, our truck began acting up. Parker brought it in to the mechanic, who told him, "This car is dead and un-drivable." At this point, this was the only vehicle our family had. I started to laugh and ask God, "What the heck is going on?" I texted a small group of people I trusted to pray because we were then out of home, in a hotel, living off chicken Caesar salads, and now had no mode of transportation. That Friday on the beach, we saw hundreds of people make a decision to follow Jesus.

God was moving.

So was satan.

God told me, "Jessi, do not post on social media what is going on. Do not glorify the attack. Keep thankfulness and praise on your lips. Do not partner with self-pity."

I wanted to go on and on about how hard everything was. I mean, I had a three-month-old baby and two toddlers sleeping in a hotel room with me. My quiet time was shredded to pieces when I needed it the most. All routine, rhythms, and semblance of peace had an atomic bomb set to it.

We laughed and just praised God for what He was doing and that we were getting to be used by Him in California.

Each Saturday morning, I woke up to *thousands* of comments, emails, and Instagram stories slandering me, my family, and our ministry. Accounts were created calling me a cult leader and the next Jim Jones. Churches ripped us apart. Christians called us "super virus spreaders" and murderers. Everything in me wanted to be understood.

I'll be honest, I am in nursery school when it comes to understanding the demonic realm. However, I will tell you this—God will bring in reinforcements where you are ill-equipped. If you keep thankfulness on your lips and your face pointed toward Him, He truly will provide all that you need.

I have always read Philippians 4:19, "And my God will fully supply your every need according to his glorious riches in the Messiah Jesus" (ISV), and thought it was simply about finances. I didn't realize that God meant He will fully supply your *every* need. More often than not, that need is people.

Inviting people and the angelic into our lives adds another layer of covering, safety, and protection as we venture out into the front lines where God is calling us to release His glory.

Pay attention to the ways the enemy is attacking you, the lies that you hear, the ways that you feel discouraged. Where is joy being robbed? As I am writing this chapter and seeking God on next steps, do you see another clue? The attacks in our house for two consecutive summers—*fire and water*. The lies are clues!

CHAPTER 17

Rumors of War

Keep your head up, he said, you are a lion,
don't forget that and neither will the sheep.
—Atticus

After the beach revivals in the summer of 2020, I kept hearing reports about the flourishing New Age movement happening in Santa Cruz, and that only 3 percent of that city was Christian. We decided to plan a "mission trip" to Santa Cruz and invite others to join us. My friend Kris Kildosher was living there at the time and told us that on Halloween, the satanic temple hosted "unbaptisms." To me, this seemed like a clear sign of what weekend we needed to be there.

Once we said "Yes" to God to move forward with the trip, we got hit hard spiritually. Doubt, fear, insecurity, drama, and confusion surrounded me like a giant cloud. I got sick with the flu and was stuck in bed for a week. Our core team was struggling to get on the same page with next steps, and I wanted to quit several times.

While the spiritual attacks and confusion with the team created so much emotional turmoil within me, our family was also being covered with incredible miracle blessings. About ten different miracles came together that orchestrated the ability for us to purchase a new truck and a second vehicle. This would be the first time our family would have two cars (with three kids)! I was able to get my "dream" car, a used white Jeep Wrangler with a tan leather interior. That same month, I also signed a contract for a book deal (this book!), which was a promise God had given me ten years ago!

As we entered into October, my friend Jen Miskov sent me a text message asking if I wanted to come with her to the Bonnie Brae House, which is the site where the Azusa Street Revival was birthed by William J. Seymour in 1906. Prophet and intercessor Lou Engle was going to be speaking there with a small group of people, and I was excited for the opportunity to meet him, listen to what he was hearing from God, and finally visit the house "behind the gate" of the Azusa landmark.

I quickly texted, "*Yes!*"

Parker agreed to watch the kids and I moved around all of my work to free up the entire day. That Monday, Jen and I drove up to L.A. in my new Jeep. As we drove up the 405 freeway and made our way to West-lake, I vented to Jen everything that was going on in my heart. It is so important to have a small group of people you can be completely transparent with, to share how you are *really* doing. I told her that I just felt so confused. I didn't know how we were going to minister in Santa Cruz without a team. Our intercessors from this summer were no longer able to come up the coast with us, and I felt like this was a *huge* hole in our "spiritual armor." We talked about revival history, and she reassured me that everything I was experiencing was actually quite normal. I shared with her that this past month I felt like I had been mentored by Charles G. Finney. His book *Revivals of Religion* was truly guiding me in the unknown territory of revival. In some ways, he felt like a spiritual father to me.

We arrived at the Bonnie Brae House and it was powerful! I loved being on the site and could feel the tangible presence of God. Lou Engle spoke to the small group of us sitting under the tent, avoiding the blazing sun, and clinging to his every word. We joined hands together and prayed, prayed for the nation, for God's will to be done, and for revival. As we contended, I prayed in repentance about abortion in our nation. After prayer was finished, Lou and one of his disciples, Mando, called Jen and me over to connect. We talked a bit about what the Lord was doing, I shared my experiences from the summer beach revival, and we prayed together. Afterward, Mando invited all of us to his house for lunch, and then to HRock Church that evening, where they would be launching a new prayer movement that night.

I called Parker and told him I really felt like he needed to be there and to join me ASAP! He quickly found a sitter (life with three kids, y'all!) and drove up and met us at Mando's house in Pasadena. We gathered around a few tables and enjoyed warm soup and sandwiches. Mando's house was full of activity! Missionaries and students came in and out, children ran up and down the stairs, people gathered on couches engaged in deep conversation, and I quietly sat at the table nibbling the turkey that peeked out of the edge of my French roll.

Mando sat on one side of me and Jen on the other. We shared stories of our experiences, the normal "background" information, and so forth. Then Mando explained to me more about the ministry he was leading called Ekballo. They called it Ekballo because Jesus uses the word *ekballo* in Matthew 9:38, where He begs His disciples to "pray to the Lord of the harvest to *send forth* (in Greek, *ekballo*) laborers into the harvest field." *Ekballo* is not the normal term used for "send," as most of our translations have it. It is a spiritually violent word filled with passion and force. It means to thrust out. It is the same word Jesus used when He said, "If I cast out (*ekballo*) demons by the finger of God, then the kingdom of God has come upon you" (Luke 11:20 NASB).

Then, something crazy happened.

Mando explained that their ministry was specifically focused on intercession for harvest. He felt like he was the Nash to a Finney. Daniel Nash was an intercessor and co-laborer of revival with Charles Finney in the early 1800s. He would partner through prayer and intercession ahead of time in the cities where Finney would host revival meetings.

I looked at Jen in shock and said nothing. I could feel that God was giving me a little hint that He had heard my prayers!

GOD WITH US

Later that afternoon, Lou asked Parker and me to share with the Ekballo team what we had been experiencing regarding revival. As we began, I felt the Holy Spirit prompting me to share with them about our vision for Santa Cruz. We wanted to win *all* of California, and we needed to strike the enemy at the source.

Lou sat at attention and began rocking back and forth in his chair. Lou's voice is raspy but powerful, and when he speaks it sounds like thunder.

After hearing about our vision to go to Santa Cruz, Lou turned to Mando and said, "Mando, I think you are supposed to join with them! I think you are to link arms!"

Mando looked to the team and asked if they wanted to go, and everyone in the room said, "*Yes!*" Mando linked arms with Parker on one side and me on the other, with Joel the worship leader for Ekballo on the other side me. The rest of the Ekballo team linked arms together with us and prayed for California.

In a moment, God had orchestrated an intercessor movement for us to link arms with and saturate Santa Cruz with the Gospel. It was the "I'm with you" moment that I needed from God to move forward!

MISSION TRIP

Over the summer, we met an incredible couple from Santa Cruz, Logan and Kerri Rooney. We had connected originally on Instagram, and they drove down to the beach revivals in July. After several conversations, we were in the process of helping them launch a Salt micro church in their area. They were both fired up to share the Gospel on the streets, make disciples, move in power, and partner with God's plans for Santa Cruz!

About two weeks before the trip, miraculous provision came in! One donor had sent us money and we were able to rent a magnificent house right on the beach that could sleep a whole group of us and serve as a "home base."

Over the five days in Santa Cruz, it was intense. Over 30 people gathered in our rental home to pray, be trained, and go out to share the Gospel. I have never witnessed so many deliverances happen in one weekend! Our team had the opportunity to visit Yonngi Cho's "Prayer Mountain" where Mando led us in prayer and declarations over the region. You could feel everything shifting. I did a quick training on deliverance and evangelism and then we hit the streets in small teams of three to four people. Demons were being provoked and cast out, people were having encounters with Jesus on the street, getting healed, and ultimately getting saved! We all came back to the house, gathered over pizza, and shared testimonies of what God had done. After everyone had left, Kerri brought over a girl who had been tormented demonically and was having several physical issues. Kendra, Vic, Mavis, Taylor, Kerri and I prayed with her for several hours and she was delivered and healed in the living room!

The night before Halloween, we partnered with Kevin and Theresa Dedmon on the wharf. They led a creative arts evangelism outreach and treasure hunt. They gave us so many incredible tools, and I couldn't believe how well they worked. Victoria and I walked up and down the boardwalk. As we gave away pictures with prophetic words, we got to lead one person after another into a relationship with Jesus.

Joel led worship right there on the edge of the beach. We had people painting, interpreting tattoos, giving away prophetic words, and more! Several members of the Ekballo team came rushing over with reports of sharing the Gospel and leading people into salvation. Kris Kildosher shared the Gospel and about 15 people raised their hands to begin following Jesus. *This was crazy!* In a place where 3 percent of the population is Christian, we were seeing a whole group of people turning to Jesus right there on the wharf. It was, indeed, *harvest season!*

This was very likely my favorite weekend of ministry since living in California. I could feel deep within my spirit how much my soul needed the refreshment of being among the lost. I know it sounds strange, but as an evangelist, at times, Christian environments can become very exhausting. I come *alive* when I am around people who are living in darkness, and I am filled with expectancy for them to encounter God! I love being a small part of bringing light into dark places and witnessing God's Kingdom realm truly invade earth!

DEMONS, SATANIC TEMPLES, AND SICKNESS—OH, MY

I jumped on Facebook and I discovered that the satanic temple decided to postpone their "unbaptism" event that was originally planned for Halloween! To me and the team, this was a great victory! We were shifting the spiritual environment!

After the street outreach, our new friend Jesse West hosted a revival night at Convergence Santa Cruz. I was tired from ministering but felt like the Lord wanted me to be there. Kris was speaking that night and out of nowhere decided to take an offering for us. He asked everyone to pray and place the money at our feet. As people came over and dropped nickels, dimes, and dollars, the Spirit of God washed over me, and I started to uncontrollably weep. Like, ugly-snot-cry. The amount given was the exact amount we needed to be able to pay our rent that month!

Saturday evening was Halloween. I felt physically exhausted. I was up all night nursing Summer, as she wasn't sleeping well during our trip. As the teams went out for street ministry, I felt like I needed to stay back and take a short nap. Later that evening, Victoria, Kendra, and I joined the teams on Main Street in downtown. The streets were *filled* with the occult. Within a matter of ten minutes, I saw several people manifesting demonically. What was so incredible is that it didn't seem to throw *anyone* off! Theresa told me story after story of good reports of people who had seen a painting and got a touch from Heaven. Kris and Joe stood on the corner and shared stories of baptisms from that day, deliverances, and spiritual showdowns. As we talked, a parade of people dressed in demon costumes marched by. This whole week was so bizarre! It was as if they took the stories of Elijah and applied these to a modern-day theme and made a movie titled *The Prophetic Showdown!*

SPECIAL OPS

That evening, I started to feel very sick. The next day, I woke up with an extremely high fever and unable to keep my eyes open. We had plans to head to San Francisco to minister, and yet I could not get out of bed—

my entire body ached. I could not eat a thing, and my fever continued to climb. Parker decided to load us all up in the car with the kids and drive back to Orange County.

As we checked out of our place in Santa Cruz, I texted Joanne, Tracy, and my friend Ana Werner who is a seer. I asked them to pray and told them that I was feeling violently sick and not able to go to San Francisco. As we drove out of Santa Cruz, Ana left me a voice memo. On the voice memo, she prayed for me to be healed and said that she saw a "spirit of offense" that may have "slimed me" during ministry. She encouraged that I should pray to just command it to go. I told Parker, and he began to pray for me as we drove onto US Highway 1. As he prayed, I felt a tightening around my throat. All of a sudden, my mind was flooded with thoughts like, *No one cares about me,*" "*I am all alone,*" "*I laid in bed sick all day and no one prayed for me.* Parker said, "Jess, command the spirit of offense to go right now!" I closed my eyes tightly as the grip around my throat got tighter. I couldn't get the words out as burning hot tears streamed down my face. My fever rose and my entire body shook. Parker put his hand on my head and declared, "Spirit of offense, I command you to *go!* Holy Spirit, fill this car with Your presence!"

I felt a giant release and shift and was able to take a breath. I looked up at Parker, sweat soaking the edges of my face, and said, "Babe, we need to figure this out. We can't keep going into the fight blind."

The following week, back in our home, I turned on the fireplace in our living room and took out a small notebook. I scribbled on the front, "Strategies for War." We then wrote down a few strategies that the Holy Spirit was showing us—how to rest, prioritizing the secret place, silencing the noise, discerning who to allow to speak into what areas, preventing false prophets from having authority at our events, and so on. I texted Ana and thanked her for what she shared the week prior. She then texted me and said while worshiping in church the Lord said, "Pray for Jessi, pray for strategy." I sat in awe; we were home working on that very thing.

Later that day, Ana left me another voice memo. (Listen, that's how you gotta roll sometimes when you both are in full-time ministry with kids!) She mentioned to me that some ministry leaders have what they call a special ops team. A team of trusted prophets, seers, and intercessors they could call upon before engaging in bigger ministry events and other assignments.

Immediately, I knew we had to pray into this. This was what we needed. Over the summer, we received a few hundred prophecies. Some words were very encouraging, some mentioned what we should do with Saturate and how God was using us, others were very confusing and sowed fear, doubt, and discord. As a reaction, I shut down the prophetic words that were coming in and had my friend collect them and put them in a separate Google Drive folder.

As Parker and I prayed together over three weeks, God highlighted to us eight people. We reached out to them individually, and each one prayed and then agreed to join our humble "special ops" team.

VICTORY

Here is my insight when it comes to spiritual warfare and revival—don't get overwhelmed by what you don't know. Keep your eyes focused on the Victor. Jesus has defeated satan. Our victory over every evil and demonic thing is in *Him*. Stay humble and keep learning. Ask God to show you what books to read. (This past summer I picked up books on seer gifts, prophetic witchcraft, discernment, and old revival books.) *Then finally, ask God who you can trust.*

The enemy will try to take you out if you isolate yourself. There needs to be people who can call out blind spots, areas where offense or bitterness or pride has snuck in. (It happens to us all!) You need people who can say "no" to you or "wait."

Over lunch one afternoon with Parker and me, Jeremy Riddle said, "Momentum is a terrible leader." I couldn't agree more, and I felt like he put to words something we were so often trying to explain to people. There were many times this summer when the crowd "demanded" we keep going or do one thing or another. Our job isn't to listen to the crowds or to react to the attacks of the enemy. Our job is to keep our hearts fleshy, forgive quickly, seek God, and ask *Him*, "Lord, what do *You* want? What are You doing? Lead me, protect me, and show me who I should partner with in this."

He will speak to you.

CHAPTER 18

Snares

What a plot twist you were.
—faraway

I feel like I'm in an intense revival boot camp," I said to Taylor, Victoria, and Kendra. It was early, around 6 a.m., and we sat curled up on my huge, gray L-shaped couch covered in blankets. I decided to put the fireplace on that morning, because it was one of those cooler, moodier California mornings.

We had moved our discipleship meetings from Tuesday nights to Thursday mornings because everyone's schedules had gotten a bit crazier since the beach revivals that summer. Taylor wrapped her fingers around the cream-colored ceramic mug with cool retro red, blue, and yellow stripes on the bottom that I found at Goodwill. That's Taylor's favorite mug to use whenever she comes over and drinks all of our coffee. She peered at me and said, "What are the biggest things that you think stop revival?" This was a very Taylor-esque question because she could tell that my mind was spinning on the subject.

Victoria then chimed in, "Yeah, yeah...like—can you miss a revival happening right in front of you?" I stared at the flames in the fireplace, watching each ember slowly flicker, pop, and ignite the flame next to it.

I lifted my eyes and returned to the conversation. I replied softly, to not wake my three sleeping children, "Fear of man, false humility, and hyper-spiritualization."

I placed my large coffee mug on the mantle, grabbed my rattan journal, and penned these three points onto the unlined pages. Kendra took out her notebook and wrote them down as well (Kendra is the best note taker in the group!) and then said, "Interesting...why those three?"

FEAR OF MAN

There is a popular quote that I have recently grown to love. Oswald Chambers said, "The frontiers of the Kingdom of God were never advanced by men and women of caution." The reality is, culture is typically Kingdom adverse (until awakening fully comes)! I believe that the words of Paul to his disciple Timothy could not be *more* relevant for today.

Paul says in Second Timothy 3:1-7:

> *But you need to be aware that in the final days* **the culture of society will become extremely fierce and difficult for the people of God.** *People will be self-centered lovers of themselves and obsessed with money. They will boast of great things as they strut around in their arrogant pride and mock all that is right. They will ignore their own families. They will be ungrateful and ungodly.*
>
> *They will become addicted to hateful and malicious slander. Slaves to their desires, they will be ferocious, belligerent haters of what is good and right. With brutal treachery, they will act*

without restraint, bigoted and wrapped in clouds of their conceit. They will find their delight in the pleasures of this world more than the pleasures of the loving God.

They may pretend to have a respect for God, but in reality they want nothing to do with God's power. *Stay away from people like these! For they are the ones who worm their way into the hearts of vulnerable women, spending the night with those who are captured by their lusts and steeped in sin. They are always learning but never discover the revelation-knowledge of truth* (TPT).

If you need a prophetic word for now, this is it.

Paul wrote to Timothy that in the final days, this is what we would see. If you read any former writings by revivalists, they are saying the same thing. Heck, if we could take these words and address this in the Church, we would see so many problems solved!

You see, the reason why we can't fear man, why we can't live to please people, is because we are *meant* to bring the opposite of what culture so readily accepts. The world is addicted to hateful and malicious slander, so it is actually *counter cultural* and offensive to speak hope despite all circumstances.

Are there any other people pleasers out there?

No? Okay, well this was the primary thing I struggled with for the majority of my life.

I feared man.

I hated confrontation.

All I wanted was to fit in and go with the status quo.

Over the last six years, it was really brought to my attention. Often-times, we relegate our need for freedom to be attached to areas such as shame, fear, anger, abuse, and the list could go on. It almost seems strange and unnatural to need "freedom" from the desire to make others happy.

I remember sitting in a cold cafe in downtown Manhattan in 2014, just recently married to Parker, who doesn't struggle with fear of man in the tiniest way. I scribbled on my journal page, "Shouldn't we want people to be happy? What's wrong with considering others' opinions first?"

The truth is, being kind and creating moments of happiness for others *is a good thing.* I especially love doing little things for my husband that make him feel loved. Parker is what you would refer to as a "wilderness lover" and loves camping, exploring, and being cold in a tent. I much more prefer sandy beaches, white sheets, ocean views, and farm-to-table dinners. So when I obliged to go camping with my husband for our family vacation, he was shocked and overjoyed. If you are a Christian, Jesus calls you to live an unselfish life, give sacrificially, and love others radically. Let's be clear, though—people pleasing is something entirely different from sacrificially loving.

PEOPLE PLEASING

As I wrestled with the tension of people pleasing and sacrificially loving others, it became crystal clear—people pleasing is a pressure to perform in exchange for love and acceptance. It's a deep desire to be accepted and receive the approval of others.

I've spoken to a lot of friends and leaders on the topic of people pleasing. The general consensus is, "You should not live to try to make people happy," and we can all agree that in some way this is not good for you. However, as I dug deeper into the core of why we people please, I realized that not only is people pleasing "bad" for you—*it is the death of you!*

Woah, woah, Jessi—that seems a little extreme.

Well, just wait.

I believe that if you are constantly living for the approval of others, it is the slow death of who God created you to be. There is a beautiful tension of being fully loved by Jesus while obeying Him and being transformed by the Holy Spirit that shapes us into the person we truly are.

If you are trying to make people happy, you are not truly serving God.

Paul says in Galatians 1:10, "Am I now trying to win the approval of human beings, or of God? Or am I trying to please people? If I were still trying to please people, I would not be a servant of Christ."

Sometimes I read the Bible and think, *Is it really saying that? Can God say that? It is so blunt.*

When I read this verse, it truly changed everything for me. The verse *does not* say, "Do not try to seek the approval of man and God because it will make you stressed and is bad for you." How often do we interpret the Scripture this way? Paul is saying that these two lifestyles are in *direct opposition* of each other. You cannot be a servant of Christ and seek the approval of man. Period. But why is this such a big deal?

Jesus as Lord

I've come to discover that there is a major difference between Jesus being your Savior and Him also being your Lord. Many of us have lifted up our hands to receive the forgiveness of our sins and receive the grace of salvation. The relentless love of God is an overwhelming gift that we receive, and we will spend all of eternity discovering the love that God has for us.

One of my favorite verses is Romans 10:9: "If you declare with your mouth, '*Jesus is Lord*,' and believe in your heart that God raised him from the dead, you will be saved." So many of us know this Scripture by heart, but we miss a glaring piece of the puzzle.

Declaring with our mouth, "Jesus is Lord," means that you are relinquishing control of your life. It means that Jesus is now in charge. The Greek word for *Lord* in this verse is *kurioj*, which is from *kuros* (supremacy); supreme in authority, by implication, Master (as a respectful title), God. The issue here is, when we are living for the approval of others, we are no longer living with Jesus being the Lord of our lives.

Why does this matter?

One practical example is that God may ask you to do something that makes others uncomfortable.

Can you believe it? God is actually not concerned with your comfort and how everyone may perceive you. If you want to advance the Kingdom and make a difference in the world, there may be times when He requires you to be countercultural. He may ask you to do something that everyone else thinks is wrong. Like, let's just say, lead a beach revival during a global pandemic when the government has essentially shut down all gatherings. Still don't believe me? You can pick up your Bible and open almost any page and see God calling people into a new life that often the "crowd" sees as wrong or too extreme.

They May Not Like You

For the time will come when people will not put up with sound doctrine. Instead, to suit their own desires, they will gather around them a great number of teachers to say what their itching ears want to hear. They will turn their ears away from the truth and turn aside to myths (2 Timothy 4:3-4).

This is an especially hard verse for anyone in public ministry. As a preacher, in my flesh I naturally want people to respond and receive my message. I was recently speaking at a conference and felt a tension between preaching a message that would make the crowd go wild or preaching the message that God wanted them to hear that would convict them but potentially change their life. When we read the Gospels, we can see that after three years of ministry, the very large crowds that followed Jesus began to thin out and actually oppose Him. His messages were sometimes seen as offensive to the general public.

As a society today, we love the quotes and Instagram images that make us feel good. All day, we share the prophetic words about how we are anointed, going to change the world, that "this is our year," and unfollow accounts that call out the sin we are living in. We follow people who can validate our need to pursue selfish ambitions and justify compromising from the laid-down life of following Jesus. Yet Second Timothy says there is a time when people will want to suit their own passions rather than hear the truth of God.

If you are living to make the crowd happy, how can you be used by God? Forget the crowd. If you are living to gain approval from anyone else but God, you start to enter into a dangerous territory that temporarily satisfies but leaves you desperate and craving more validation and affirmation. The Christian who needs the approval of a stranger will never be the salt and light they were designed to be.

So what can you do?

Platform Heart Check

Unfortunately, I think freedom from this area of people pleasing is a process and there is no "anti-people pleasing" magic pill. Over the last few years, I have found that it requires daily choosing to ask God to help me surrender my will and any need for affirmation. The truth is, approval is actually addicting. Like any addiction, it takes intention to break its effects. As much as we all love social media, it is like the very heroin needle sticking out of our arm waiting for another shot.

About every month or so, I do a platform heart check. I know this sounds funny, but I think it is important to bring the hidden areas of our lives to God in an honest way. I ask God to show me areas where I preferred the approval of people over what God was asking me to do or say. What ways does God want me to use the platforms I have?

While going through this process, I think it is important to surround ourselves with people who are following Jesus and can speak life into us when the crowds don't.

I encourage you to meditate on the Scriptures in Galatians and know what the Bible says about serving God and living a free life in the Spirit. I pray that as you get free in this area, the Holy Spirit will add to your faith and give you the boldness and courage to fully surrender to Him and live fully alive for the audience of One. We need prophetic voices who are not silent out of fear of losing followers. We need to get over how we will be perceived. We have no control over what others might think, and we will likely be perceived wrong anyway!

This isn't the hour to play small. Right now, in Jesus' name, we rebuke the fear of man, false humility, and hyper-spiritualization.

FALSE HUMILITY

I don't have time to dive into the depths of false humility and hyper-spiritualization, but I pray that you can open up these potential blind spots to the Holy Spirit to search deep within you. Here is the thing—birthing and sustaining the things God has given you requires complete yieldeness to God. Period.

False humility will take you out because it is a form of pride. As you lead, everyone and their mother will want to tell you who you are, what you are supposed to do, and how you are supposed to do it. *I am not even joking.* I thought my identity was pretty secure before we began leading Saturate, but I didn't realize how often and quickly the enemy would sow in seeds of doubt.

I would find myself in moments when a well-known Christian leader would say something like, "God is using you in revival. Do you know what He is calling you to do?"

In a desire to remain humble, I would say things like, "I don't know." That was a lie, and the Lord would lead me privately to repent. I would hear Him say, "Don't pretend like you don't know who you are or what you are called to do. That is false humility."

Ouch.

My friend Trish has been really helpful in this area. When I would feel insecure, she would just be that voice I needed to remind me to "not play small." That I was living as Jessi fully alive. That I had permission to celebrate all that God was doing. That there are years of deep work I have done in secret and didn't "stumble upon" revival. That what looks like a "suddenly" to everyone else was years of believing God, obeying, sacrificing, and stepping out in risk.

The reality is, there are so many critics in the world. There will be people who say that they are "championing you" and the calling on your life. My earnest advice is—*watch the fruit.* If it feels like some of the people in your life can't celebrate a win and you feel false humility creeping in, pay attention!

HYPER-SPIRITUALIZATION

Nothing will snuff out the wildfire of revival more effectively than hyper-spiritualization! No Jezebel spirit, demonic principality, or false prophet is more effective at shutting down revival than the sneaky behavior of hyper-spiritualization.

Over the last few years, I have watched so many pastors not engage in the current harvest out of a belief that it was going to look a different way. I have seen so many people, passionate about revival, never leave the prayer closet as revival is roaring through the region.

You want to know how many times every revivalist felt like leading revival all the time? *Never.*

The reality is, your feelings are not your ruler; Jesus is.

If God has told you to do something, then do it.

I need to say this as clear as I can. *You can't mess up God's will for your life by trying to do God's will!*

I have spoken to so many millennials about their calling and purpose. As they are waiting on God, they are stuck at a yellow light. Always requesting prophetic insight, never acting. It's as though our cars, driving down the road of revival, have gotten stuck at yellow. While you wait on the Lord, you can confidently continue to do the things He laid out simply in Scripture.

Here's my quick Revival 101 school:

+ Follow Jesus.
+ Read the Bible.
+ Be filled with the Holy Spirit.
+ Preach the Gospel.

+ Make disciples.

+ Give generously.

+ Repent quickly.

+ Commit yourself to other believers.

+ If you ever hear the "spirit" telling you not to do any of these things, command satan to flee from you in Jesus' name!

And for the love of God—like, literally, the love of God—*let your yes be yes and your no be no.* So often, in charismatic Christian cultures, we have "hyper-spiritualized" not making plans. I believe that this is the hour that the Lord is calling us into the prayer closet for strategies of war to go out and win nations through the power of the Gospel and discipleship. Walking around aimlessly, committing to things and bailing out, not having a plan or strategy doesn't make you more Spirit-led; it makes you lazy and often confused. It makes you hard to depend on and partner with. We need to stop exalting chaos as a marker of holiness.

Selah.

Killing the People Pleaser

Running around and trying to be on time to appease people vs. God

Preaching for crowd / leaders approval — earn my "platform" time through performance.
 — punished — taken off platform

What people may think on social —
Beach photos
politics
Appeasing to everyones offense

Pendulum swing — losing my gift of compassion
Zero F's (college kids)

fear of rejection
fear of losing / messing up my calling

Nightlife
 ⤷ look a certain way / act a certain way
 is the church the same?

PART 5

If Not Now, Then When?

> *I baptize you with water for repentance. But after me comes one who is more powerful than I, whose sandals I am not worthy to carry. He will baptize you with the Holy Spirit and fire.*
>
> **—Matthew 3:11**

Excerpt of *Lectures on Revival of Religion* by Charles Finney.

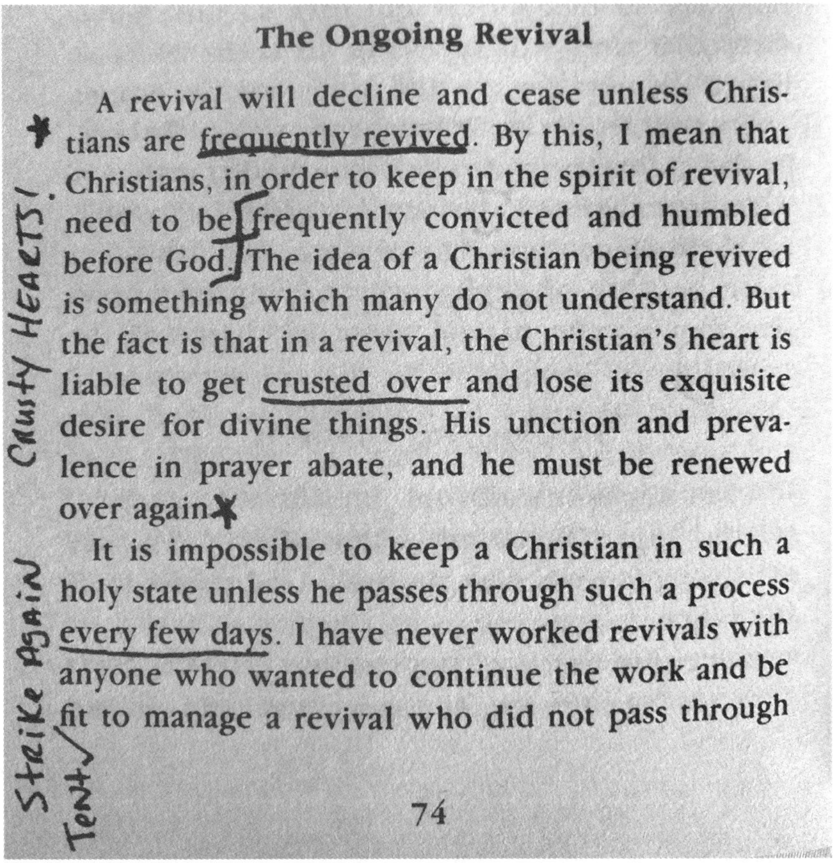

The Ongoing Revival

A revival will decline and cease unless Christians are frequently revived. By this, I mean that Christians, in order to keep in the spirit of revival, need to be frequently convicted and humbled before God. The idea of a Christian being revived is something which many do not understand. But the fact is that in a revival, the Christian's heart is liable to get crusted over and lose its exquisite desire for divine things. His unction and prevalence in prayer abate, and he must be renewed over again.

It is impossible to keep a Christian in such a holy state unless he passes through such a process every few days. I have never worked revivals with anyone who wanted to continue the work and be fit to manage a revival who did not pass through

74

[handwritten marginalia: "CRUSTY HEARTS!" "Strike Again" "Tent"]

CHAPTER 19

Keepin' It Real

Stones taught me to fly
Love, it taught me to lie
Life, it taught me to die
So it's not hard to fall
When you float like a cannonball
—**Damien Rice**, "Cannonball"

I don't want to write this chapter."

These were literally my first thoughts as I sat down to write this section. I wondered, *How could life be accelerating with so many promises being fulfilled and yet at the same time be intertwined with so much pain, confusion, and purging of my soul?*

To be honest, I still have not quite processed all that has happened this past summer of 2020. I know what you're thinking: *Didn't you just write a whole book about it?* Yet when you are living in the "now and not yet" of so many prophecies, promises, and still gripping faith like a cold metal bar on a looping roller coaster, it becomes hard to recognize the difference between the vision and reality when it is *actually happening.* As I mentioned earlier, the crowds, our friends, and even the press requested that we keep moving forward that summer. The secular news outlets, like the LA Times, were actually on our side and asking to cover the "revival in California"! However, in the quiet, silent times alone with God, I deeply knew that it was time to pause. This was one of the hardest decisions I had to make in my life.

IN THE PROCESS

I had always dreamed of writing a book one day. I absolutely love written words, and my collection of books is my greatest treasure. I keep old used books on revival on my vanity next to my bed and often turn to the pages for encouragement and instruction. Many times, I feel like I am being mentored by revivalists who are no longer alive through their written words. So often, I have wished that I could pick up a phone, call Charles G. Finney, and ask, "What did you do when no one wanted to help you? How did you feel in that moment? How did you become so 'on fire' for God?" Words have tremendous power, and the responsibility to write and create, I didn't take lightly.

Through several divine moments, I was connected to the team at Destiny Image. As I spoke to my publisher Larry, I believed God was asking me to write a book while *in* revival. You see, so many of the revival books that you can find in your local bookstore are history books. They typically are written *after* the revival has come and gone.

I thought—what if Charles Finney, John Wesley, or William J. Seymour had written books about their *process* in the midst of leading revival? What if we could learn, firsthand, what they were learning and experiencing while leading, pioneering, or overcoming trials during revival? I think that is why so many of us love the Psalms so much. It's gritty, raw, and we get an inside look into how David really felt while in the process of becoming the person God had anointed him to be.

Aren't we all in this ongoing process of transformation, living in a moving picture? Although it is uncomfortable, I believe that I needed to share with you these tools and lessons that are too big for a social media post. I need to bring you in, so that when you step into what God has called you to, you don't get taken out!

> *Be sober [well balanced and self-disciplined], be alert and cautious at all times. That enemy of yours, the devil, prowls around like a roaring lion [fiercely hungry], seeking someone to devour* (1 Peter 5:8 AMP).

So often, we want to share the highlight reel. I want to celebrate all of the wins of what God *has done* and what He is *currently doing*. As I write these words, we are *in* revival. However, I have experienced the many ways the enemy has tried to take me out this last year. Even now, I am wrestling with so many next steps being presented before us. I want to take you deeper into my process of what I was feeling in the midst of everything that was going on during that season. In the pages that follow, I open up my journal to share with you the very real struggles I came up against. I hope these insights into my then reality will encourage you to know that when God is leading you outside of your comfort zone to continue to press in and follow Him, He will never let you down. This last year, I have truly had to find my shelter in Him.

> *He who dwells in the secret place of the Most High shall abide under the shadow of the Almighty. I will say of the Lord, "He is my refuge and my fortress; my God, in Him I will trust." Surely*

He shall deliver you from the snare of the fowler and from the perilous pestilence (Psalm 91:1-3 NKJV).

The following are some of the journal entries I wrote during this season of pioneering revival and what I was processing in the aftermath of the beach revival.

August 20, 2020

To be honest, I need fresh vision. I feel like I can only be radically obedient if I could *see* first what the Father was doing.

We organized a retreat with a few of our core team members from the beach revivals, mainly to connect on a deeper level and dream together. I could sense God giving Parker and me increased spiritual "authority" in California. We had received so many prophetic words regarding wildfires going up and down the coast that the only logical thing was to make a strategy to take Saturate on the road. I have written plans, then scratched out plans, then made new plans, then scratched them out again. Different team members are emailing me, texting, and asking, "What's next?"

I don't really know.

In a period of six weeks, we saw thousands of people get saved and baptized. They came to the beach not to see a famous preacher (I am not offended, ha ha!) but to encounter God. The region had shifted, and it seemed like baptisms had become a priority in churches and other ministries! People are baptizing people everywhere! Victory!

I keep hearing the Lord say, "If not now, when?"

So much is happening. All at once!

"What makes a Saturate event?"

+ Intercession / prayer strikes
+ Secret place leads to Spirit-led leadership
+ Different giftings converging
+ Gospel being preached is the main event
+ Baptism in water and fire
+ People need to be commissioned to go
+ Only partner with churches that will make disciples

I feel a draw to be on the road as we prayed about what cities needed to be ignited. Our emails are flooded with invitations, but I want to see California saved and the idea is burning within me.

September 8, 2020

Right now I am praying and fasting regarding the next steps. We have some places, dates mapped out—Santa Cruz, Slo, Malibu, etc. but I'm just confused at what the next steps are. Currently, there are "actual wildfires" spreading across California. I am trying to discern my role and vision in all of this. I am trying to release the other tasks and roles to team members and give away authority for Saturate, but people keep dropping the ball and I don't really feel like they are "all in."

Mandate: ignite fires

We ended up hosting a prayer night with key people involved with Saturate in our home. There are so many themes, ideas, and honestly, so many different agendas. Where do I begin? I feel like again, the plans need to change. God is calling our family to be missionaries to California. I keep hearing Santa Cruz, to cut off the enemy at the source. To bring the Gospel where there has been so much witchcraft. I believe we are supposed to have a mission field focus for a few months.

September 15, 2020

Honestly, I am so tired and I want to quit. The drama is taking me out emotionally. I feel like we defeated so much opposition already between demonic attacks on the street, the police coming to our house, thousands of social media accusations, churches calling us rebellious, our house construction having us out of our home for eight weeks, our car dying—yet we persevered!

So many of our team members who said they were coming on the road are no longer coming for various reasons. I keep hearing that age-old lie, "you are all alone." The lie feels real.

I just started to read *Discerning Prophetic Witchcraft* by Jennifer LeClaire. This summer, this felt like a total blind area for me. So many agendas, weird passive-aggressive messages, and just strange behavior and manipulation came to the surface. I feel like my friend group has shrunk as I try to discern who I can actually trust. It feels so weird. God, what are You teaching me? I can feel a greater dependence on You. I feel like I am on a great adventure but also feel so alone and scared.

I believe God showed me that in December we will see Orange County saved. A tent revival maybe? I can feel the dirt in my feet and I pray. I am reading *Revivals of Religion* by Charles Finney where he says "you should put forth effort for revivals." Sitting still is not faith. Finney writes that revivals are not miracles. Well, that's encouraging! I agree.

I am so tired of everyone acting like what happened this summer was just some sovereign act of God. I believe God wants to multiply what happened this summer, but where are the yielded ones who will partner with HIS vision for America? So many churches are preaching about revival, but so few churches want to be out on the streets or making disciples. With each new open door comes more resistance. I feel like the constant meetings, calls, and texts to explain my heart are slowing down the movement. I can feel the Lord's presence, but I just don't want to be around people anymore! Joanne called me and said she sensed the Lord is trying to protect me, it feels like the opposite! I am having a hard time navigating "who is with us" in regard to words vs. actions. I need to stop feeling guilty for being a forerunner and need to have permission to vision cast, dream, risk, and take new ground. I read this today by Finney and felt like I wasn't a crazy person....

"And yet some people are terribly alarmed at all direct efforts to promote a revival, and they cry out: 'You are trying to get up a revival in your own strength. Take care, you are interfering with the sovereignty of God. Better keep along in the usual course, and let God give a revival when He thinks it is best. God is a sovereign, and it is very wrong for you to attempt to get up a revival, just because you think a revival is needed.' This is just such preaching as the devil wants. And men cannot do the devil's work more effectually than by preaching up the sovereignty of God, as a reason why we should not put forth efforts to produce a revival."

—*Lectures on Revivals of Religion* by Charles G. Finney

October 2020

I am really struggling and want to curl up and cry and quit. I don't want to keep going. About half our team that "committed" to be on the road, wherever we would go, have now withdrawn and are no longer coming to Santa Cruz. These are the people who two months ago were "all in," wanting to sell everything to hit the road and ignite revival. It's hard to not feel rejected. It's hard to not believe the reoccurring lies. Jesus, in these moments, I really don't want to lead a ministry. I just want to spend time with You, get a normal job, and reach the lost with the girls I disciple.

I understand now why every revival in history has ended. Teams are what make a revival hard, the events themselves are easy! I feel like I'm in a web of miscommunication. I say "the sky is blue" and people hear "the sky is red."

I'm on a fast-track master class when it comes to leadership. I'm having to have hard and difficult conversations about what gossip is and what is creating division. I'm trying so hard to be vulnerable, meanwhile I feel like people aren't being honest with me. My schedule and time are so limited.

I read an excerpt from Rick Joyner's *The Final Quest*:

"The Lord continued His exhortation: 'I have given you spiritual gifts and power, and an increasing understanding of My Word and My kingdom, but the greatest weapon you have been given is the Father's love. As long as you walk in My Father's love you will never fail. The fruit of this tree is the Father's love which is manifested in Me. This love which is in Me must be your daily bread.'"

Jesus, keep my heart tender. Help me to forgive quickly. I lay everything down at Your feet. If You want me to be done with Salt Churches, Saturate, whatever…my plans are open to You Lord! Jesus, I forgive every person who has hurt me or disappointed me intentionally or unintentionally. I release them to You. Lord, please bring people into our lives whom we can run with.

December 2020

The tent revival is this weekend and I am sitting on my bed crying. I feel like everything is falling apart. Originally, the tent that was "donated" for us this summer to use is now unavailable, just a few weeks before the event. Mario Murillo offered for us to use his tent, but we are having so many logistical issues getting it here. Last week, we finally finalized that his tent is coming, and Parker is now at the field in San Juan Capistrano to meet the team and begin setup.

Last night we had a call with some of the "special ops" team. Parker's parents, Bob and Mavis, were on the call, as well as Joanne, Ana, Ryan and Tina, and Jen. Since Saturday, I have felt anxiety wash over Parker and me. It's frustrating because we typically aren't anxious people. Hotel logistics for some of the team have been a mess as we have had to book, cancel, and re-book several hotel rooms. I am trying to not feel upset when it comes to finances because I had gotten special rates on the hotel rooms during "Cyber Monday" deals and now those rates are gone. I am paying three times the price for the same room, which the "Long Islander" in me, who loves a good deal, is struggling with.

On the special ops call, Ana prayed protection over our family, specifically over the kids and their routines. She and Ryan prayed against anxiety, stress with the mechanics, and other things that were taking away our peace this week. I felt the Lord's peace as we prayed and could feel the enemy trying to entangle me into a web of decision making. I spent all afternoon at my kitchen counter with Victoria trying to figure out HDMI cables for the livestream. At this point, I don't even care if we have a livestream, I just want peace.

At around 3 a.m. last night, Ethan began coughing uncontrollably. Parker was in and out of his room throughout the night. At around 5 a.m., Ethan started screaming, "My stomach hurts, my stomach hurts!" We jumped out of bed, into his room, to find him covered in throw up and tears. We took off his pajamas, removed the bedding, and quickly put it into the washing machine. Parker lit the fire in our living room, and I held Ethan, coughing in my arms.

"I'm so tired," I whispered to Parker, as the fire warmed our living room and Parker knelt down to turn the Christmas tree on. The sun was still not up yet to beckon the beginning of the day, as we laid curled up on the couch in the still of our safe space.

Bob and Mavis came over early to help me with the kids and brought me coffee (thank You Jesus!) as I made Summer a bottle while holding Ethan in my arms. I then received a text from my best friend Trish who is helping us with logistics, "Hey Jess, can you call me really quick."

My stomach sunk. I knew something was wrong, mostly because if it were a minor thing, Trish would have just texted me. I picked up the phone and called her immediately, as Ethan continued coughing curled up in my lap.

"It looks like one of the guest speakers might have to cancel," Trish hesitantly said over the speakerphone.

Ana called me and shared what she was seeing, that the enemy was trying to attack us however he could. She prayed over Ethan and I hung up the phone. It's not even 7:30 a.m. and I feel finished with this day. I want to quit. I want to cancel the whole thing.

I went into the shower and put the water as steaming hot as I could handle. I lit a candle and turned the lights off and just cried. Sometimes, you just need to cry in the shower.

As the steam filled the bathroom, I heard a tiny knock on the door. My four-year-old David stood in the doorway with tears in his eyes. He cried out to me, "Mama, I don't want to go to school today."

Perfect.

I got out of the shower, wrapped myself in a towel, and knelt down convincing him that he had to be a big boy and go to school. I understand how he feels. I, too, want to curl up in a blanket, do normal "mom" things, get some Christmas shopping done, and escape.

I have run-sheets to finish, registrations to review, emails to send out, chairs to order, hosts to confirm, and I just don't know when or how all of this is going to get done and now I need a speaker for Saturday night. Lord, I need Your help. Please, show me what You're doing. Again, I am at the end of myself.

That was literally what was happening to me right before the tent revival and how I felt in the moments leading up it. I share my journal entries to give you some real-life examples of what it looks like in the *process* of being willing to lay down your life for revival. It may look glamorous on the outside when it's "go time," but in reality very few people understand the challenges and the cost it takes to step into that moment, let alone a lifetime of saying costly yeses to the Lord. For those who are willing to endure and not give up, they will see God do wonders.

I believe if you are reading this right now, you, too, are one of the few who are willing and ready to give your costly yes to Jesus.

CHAPTER 20

Drown

Open up my eyes and
Tell me who I am
Let me in on all your secrets
No inhibition, no sin
How deep is your love?
Is it like the ocean?
—Calvin Harris & Disciples,
"How Deep Is Your Love"

SEVEN WAVES VISION

Two weeks before we went to Santa Cruz, the Lord woke me up in the middle of the night. I saw a vision of these giant waves rolling onto the shores of California. As each wave crashed in, the waters covered the state and slowly rolled through the rest of the nation. As one wave drew back slowly, there was a pause before the next, larger wave crashed in harder and more violently.

The revival that we are currently in is similar, and yet entirely different from every revival in history. It's as though a convergence of every spiritual well dug in this world is being drawn upon, rising up, and going to smash in like a violent wave.

This is just the groundswell.

I believe we are now transitioning into the second wave of revival. If you know anything about sets of waves, they increase in size, and the last wave is absorbed by the next wave as it is drawn back out. Can you feel what the Holy Spirit is about to pour out on our nation?

I hear the Lord say, "Repent, while you can."

For years, I have felt a deep tension in church services. I sense the Lord is *done* allowing the secret sins in the Church to go on unnoticed. Let us not forget, Jesus is indeed coming back. He is coming for a pure bride! In our prayer meetings, we are asking God to reveal the hidden things in our nation, to shine a light on the darkness, and then we are shocked that He is shining that light on us first!

I cry out in prayer to the Church, "Repent! Repent while you can. Every hidden agenda is coming into the light, every secret sin. The days of favor based on 'networking' and charisma are finished!"

THE IDENTIFIERS OF THE SEVEN WAVES

In my opinion, 2020 was the beginning of the first wave of the vision, and what we saw during the beach revivals was just a birth pain of the revival that is coming forth. God is bridging the gap between denominational and generational lines in California and for the rest of the nation.

As I have prayed and pressed into this vision, I believe that each wave signified a very strategic and specific move of God for the body of consecrated believers. These are:

1. Wave One: Separating the wheat from the tares; the rise of the remnant.

2. Wave Two: The resurrection of the unborn; repentance from Moloch; rise of Esthers (women who are afraid to speak who have had abortions).

3. Wave Three: Deliverance and witchcraft; prophetic showdown.

4. Wave Four: National repentance—hidden sins exposed nationally and in churches; "repent while you can."

5. Wave Five: Cleaning up house; false prophets exposed; getting the house in order.

6. Wave Six: Tearing down / exposing all idols; a great fire.

7. Wave Seven: The recognition of Jesus as Lord; one nation *under* God. The last chance.

I need to eventually write more, breaking down and processing all that the Lord is showing me, because it needs time and accountability, but here is what I have at the moment to share:

- This "seven wave season" will span over a ten-year period. The revival will have an ebb and flow like a wave pattern, much like contractions during labor.

- The revival will not take place in one city (like Toronto). It will be led and sustained by the saints in multiple cities.

- The leaders in this end-time harvest will be those who are training and equipping others like generals in an army.

- There will be a rise of many false prophets; we need increased discernment in this hour. Don't trust words; look at the fruit.

- California will be an ignition state, and there are wildfires of movement that will happen up and down the coast that will spread across the nation into a revolution.

- Baptism in water and fire is catalytic—it is the fuel for the wildfire of revival! Baptize, baptize, baptize!

PICKUP TRUCK BAPTISMS

In September 2016, Parker and I were invited to speak at "Awakening Conference" hosted by Adventures in Missions. David was three weeks old at the time, and we had driven 27 hours from New York to Georgia to take part. It was our first time speaking at an event since coming off staff in New York. We stayed at Clint's house, and he was helping me prepare for the weekend. We sat at his kitchen table, sipping soup, and he glared up at me and said, "Jess, what do You see the Holy Spirit doing?" Clint was intense and direct.

I closed my eyes and said, "I keep hearing the Lord say, 'I'm drawing a line in the sand. In the next few years, you will know very clearly who is for Me or against Me.' He is giving everyone here an opportunity to *go all in*." I felt in my spirit that the days of being lukewarm were over for the Church in America. We needed to rise up. We needed to know the Word *and* be filled with the Holy Spirit. We needed to repent for ignoring the third person of the Trinity.

He then said, "That's good. You better do whatever He shows you." Freedom like that is nerve-wracking for a young preacher. It was the first time I was able to preach with full permission to do "whatever the Holy Spirit showed me."

As I prepared the next morning, the Lord told me that He was going to highlight the importance of baptism. That morning, I headed to the conference to preach. As I got on stage, I felt something shift. What happened next shocked me. I ended up reading one psalm in the Bible and began to weep. I couldn't get through the text. I could feel the weight of God's holiness drawing us all in. He was inviting us to purify ourselves. People began running to the front, screaming out to God for forgiveness. The founder of the organization came on stage and wept before God, asking everyone for forgiveness. After about an hour, I ended up preaching for only a few minutes and over 75 people spontaneously decided to get baptized in the back of a pickup truck. It was wild.

I believe that there is something significant about baptisms in this next move of God.

If in Joel 2 God says, "I am going to pour out my Spirit upon all flesh," the question is, is all flesh prepared for His Spirit?

I believe this baptism revival signifies more than being born again. We, as the Church, need to *drown*. We need to let the former things drown in that water. We need to let ourselves die in that water. I urge you, get baptized 1,000 times until you have died to your sinful nature and are prepared for Him to fill you with His Holy Spirit!

BORN—AGAIN!

The subject of being born again is one of the greatest passions of my life. The transition from death to life is the greatest miracle we can witness on earth. Before you see any prophecies, dreams, or callings truly develop, you need to die to yourself and be resurrected *in Him*. Galatians 3:26-27 says it this way:

> For you [who are born-again have been reborn from above— spiritually transformed, renewed, sanctified and] are all children of God [set apart for His purpose with full rights and privileges] through faith in Christ Jesus. For all of you who were baptized into Christ [into a spiritual union with the Christ, the Anointed] have clothed yourselves with Christ [that is, you have taken on His characteristics and values] (AMP).

The word *baptism* means "to plunge or immerse." When you go into those waters, something supernatural takes place. This is not just a symbol of your faith; it is *transformative*. Jesus said to the Pharisee Nicodemus: "No one can enter the kingdom of God unless they are born of water and the Spirit" (John 3:5).

Want to live a brand-new life in Jesus? You must be baptized. This is not poetry or some symbolic moment. Baptism is an actual *new birth* by water and the Holy Spirit. When you are immersed into the water, the old is gone and the new has come. A new person emerges out of the water, afresh with His Holy Spirit.

I can't begin to tell you how many people I have seen delivered of demonic strongholds during baptisms. It's like the demons can't handle the water! This is a huge reason why we drag around tubs of water or host events on the beach. I can't preach the Gospel and not have baptisms available. I simply will not refuse someone that opportunity for new life.

So many churches go back and forth about "just a sprinkle" or full immersion. I am not going to get caught up in all of that. My thought is, why settle for a sprinkle when you can be saturated?

We need to stop navigating our lives around what's okay, and we need to radically *obey*. The Church needs to cry out *"What must we do, Lord?!"*

The days have changed. It can no longer be about what we can get away with; it has to be about living a life *fully alive* and consecrated. When we are baptized, we are declaring, "It is no longer I who live, but Christ who *lives in me*."

DEEP

When Parker and I were in Australia in 2015, we were at the beach in Byron Bay. I was standing along the shore of the ocean and I couldn't see the end of it. I was up early, before the sunrise, praying, "God, I just want more of You. Holy Spirit, I want more of You. Holy Spirit. I want more, I want more."

Then I heard God say to me, "If you stepped into the middle of the ocean, would you say to the Pacific, 'I want more ocean'?" And I responded, "No."

Then He said, "It's like asking the Pacific Ocean for more ocean when you're completely surrounded and covered already by the waters."

When you're in the middle of the water, you can't ask for more; it's everywhere. It's all consuming. You have it all. The choice really is, how deep do *you* want to go?

As I stood on the shore, I looked over the hill where the lighthouse was. I could see the sun slowly rising above the edge of the sea. Little sparks of orange, red, and purple danced across the onshore waves. I had this little bit of ocean on my toes, but the whole thing was available to me if I wanted it.

Then I took a little, tiny step.

As I got in deeper, the water become colder and a little uncomfortable.

Then I went in a little bit deeper and started to feel fear creep in. "Maybe there are sharks in the water?"

As I stepped further and further in, eventually I couldn't touch my feet on the ground and I started to lose control.

SURRENDER

Psalm 42:7 says, "Deep calls to deep in the roar of your waterfalls; all your waves and breakers have swept over me."

Deep calls to deep in the oceans of Your love.

Deep calls to deep.

Not a little; God is going deep.

He's given you the depth of who He is, and He calls you deeper and deeper and deeper! So as the Church, let's stop saying, "God, we want more of You," and let's start praying, "God, You can have more of me." As we surrender our will, we will receive all that God has for us.

I believe, prophetically, we all need to drown.

Is there anything in your life that would cause you to say "no" to God? What if God wanted you to give up all your money? What if He wanted you to move? Lay down your ministry? Start a job as a receptionist? Get off social media? Engage more on social media? Not post about politics? Post more about politics?

Is every thought, passion, decision, plan, and agenda yielded to Him?

I want to tell you the hard truth. Whatever that thing is that causes you to say "no" to God is actually an idol.

We constantly have to invite the Holy Spirit to check our hearts and ask ourselves, "Is there anything that would ever cause me to say no to God?" If you feel like there is, that is a signal to show you there is fear.

There is no fear in love. But perfect love drives out fear, because fear has to do with punishment. The one who fears is not made perfect in love. We love because he first loved us (1 John 4:18-19).

As we obey God and surrender control, fear goes away and faith increases. Faith is directly attached to obedience. If He is asking you to lay something down, will you trust Him? Will you believe His love for you more than your love for you?

If you don't believe me, just read the book of James. James was Jesus' brother. Just read what he has to say about faith and what you do with it. He basically says that if you actually have faith, *you're required to do something.*

If I said to Parker, "I love you," but then I went out drinking and partying and sleeping with other guys, the reality is I don't really love him. I don't. My actions don't match up with my words.

So if we love God, we obey Him. The coolest thing about obedience is that when we understand the love God has for us, there's no obligation attached to it because we just receive more of God's love! When He calls us into obedience, it's an exciting opportunity to receive *more* of His love!

This past season, God has taught me the most significant lesson I could have ever learned:

- God is not withholding His love and power from you.
- If you want more of God, go in deeper.
- Yield to the waves.

It's about Him, being with Him, loving Him, receiving His love, partnering with Him and doing what He is doing. Although my heart feels shredded at times, I can feel the Holy Spirit wooing me in deeper. How deep will you go?

CHAPTER 21

Remnant Rising

God is not about using the mighty but the willing. He is not into using amazing people, just ones who prepared to lay their lives down to Him. God is not looking for extraordinary, exceptionally gifted people, just laid down lovers of Jesus who will carry His glory with transparency and not take it for themselves.
—Heidi Baker

Okay, this chapter may be the most controversial in the whole book. However, here is the truth. Everyone is invited to be a part of revival, but what breaks me, keeps me awake at night, is that not everyone will be a part of revival. Ugh, I hate having to even type that! I am hoping that you choose to go all in, but ultimately the choice is yours. Sorry, but I just need to say it.

Let me break this down.

There is a sketch that a very funny (non-Christian) comedian does about the movie *Man on Fire*. He is referring to the famous action movie featuring Denzel Washington. In the sketch he shares how we think we are "the man on fire." We see Denzel Washington come out of the car, dressed all cool, shoot the bad guys, and look totally calm while doing it. We are like, "Yeah, that's me, I'm that guy."

In one scene, there is a pretty average-looking guy holding a stack of papers and walking over to the copy machine. When the shooting begins, he freaks out and throws the papers in the air and frantically runs to the side avoiding the bullets. The comedian says, "You are that guy." The sketch is funny because it's kind of true. For many of us, we are not "the man on fire." When persecution, resistance, and warfare come—we flee.

You can post on your Instagram all day that you are a revivalist, but if you ain't willing to lay it all down, you ain't a revivalist. Well, at least not yet. However, I have good news.

Jesus *actually is* the Man on fire.

He didn't flee. He *chose* to go to the cross.

It gets better.

He promises us *His* Holy Spirit, so that we can also be the man on fire. In your own strength, you will throw the files in the air, you will resist persecution, you will choose comfort over obedience. However, I am going to give you *every* key that you need to resist apathy, overcome fear, and *be on fire*.

I know this is a hard word, but the reason I am sharing it is because we need the Church to rise up. When I say, "the Church" I am talking about you and me. I am talking about the everyday believers who are filing into church week in and week out and pay $30 to take a spiritual gifts assessment to then join a parking lot team. Okay, sorry for my sarcasm, but we *need* to do better.

EXPECT PERSECUTION

Jesus gives you a promise that can change the world. I can prove it. Jesus says in John 16:1-4:

All this I have told you so that you will not fall away. They will put you out of the synagogue; in fact, the time is coming when anyone who kills you will think they are offering a service to God. They will do such things because they have not known the Father or me. I have told you this, so that when their time comes you will remember that I warned you about them.

I know, I know, you are thinking, *Jessi, this is not very encouraging. Can we skip to the part where God blesses us?*

The truth is, no, we can't skip to that part. Here's why. If you want to see revival, honestly and truly, you need to know that persecution is expected.

Period.

However, Jesus promises that we can endure through persecution. Right before He tells His disciples that they can expect to possibly be killed (you don't hear that from the American pulpit!), He says to them:

If the world hates you, keep in mind that it hated me first. If you belonged to the world, it would love you as its own. As it is, you do not belong to the world, but I have chosen you out of the world. That is why the world hates you. Remember what I told you: "A servant is not greater than his master." If they persecuted me, they will persecute you also. ...When the Advocate comes, whom I will send to you from the Father—the Spirit of truth who goes out from the Father—he will testify about me. And you also must testify, for you have been with me from the beginning (John 15:18-20,26-27).

Bishop Garlington once said, "You can't preach the Gospel and not expect persecution."

Everyone in the room cheered. Yet if we put up a remotely controversial Facebook post and face a few criticisms, we quickly hit delete and hope we didn't lose too many followers in the process. Jesus didn't promise us the Holy Spirit for us to grow in popularity and sell more conference tickets! He gave us the Holy Spirit so that we would testify of God! That we would be taught by His Spirit, that we would be comforted when things are uncomfortable, and that we would have courage to continue to preach despite all circumstances, government rulings, and insecurities. Let this be the hour for the followers of Jesus to preach the Gospel at all costs!

GOD IS CALLING MISSIONARIES TO AMERICA

God is calling the missionaries to America for such a time as this. Has God recently been giving you new vision and showing you His plans for cities in America?

He may be calling you to be a missionary there!

When we moved to Orange County in 2016, the Lord said to us, "I'm calling you to be full-time missionaries." This was a strange paradigm shift for me because I always envisioned missionaries in the dirt in Africa, not on the beaches of California.

If God is highlighting a city to you, press in and obey! There is favor for you there! In Luke 1:76-79, it says:

For you will go on before the Lord to prepare the way for him, to give his people the knowledge of salvation through the forgiveness of their sins, because of the tender mercy of our God, by which the rising sun will come to us from heaven to shine on those living in darkness and in the shadow of death, to guide our feet into the path of peace.

As I have been reading and meditating on Luke, I believe that God is commissioning many to pick up the mantle of John the Baptist and wake up the sleeping Church in America.

A SLEEPING CHURCH

I grew up in the church. As a little girl, I would stand next to my mom and lift my hands in worship. I experienced the presence of God, witnessed His miraculous provision for our family, and loved singing about His transforming love and power. As I mentioned earlier, my mom was saved and immediately began an *all-in* relationship with Jesus. She had been through too much to just adopt a new set of rules through religion. She needed something that worked.

Only a resurrected Savior can actually help you thrive in the world we live in today.

My husband Parker recently shared with me an interesting statistic. Approximately 65 percent of America is considered an evangelical Christian. Yet when we watch the news, walk down the street, enter our schools it seems like the 65 percent have gone missing.

We read in Matthew an interesting story of Jesus "on His way" being interrupted by a problem. An influential Jewish leader had approached

Jesus because his daughter had just died. The streets were filled with rumors of Jesus' miraculous power and the Jewish leader was desperate. We read in Matthew 9:23-26:

> *When Jesus finally entered the home of the Jewish leader, he saw a noisy crowd of mourners, wailing and playing a funeral dirge on their flutes. He told them, "You must leave, for the little girl is not dead; she's only asleep." Then everyone began to ridicule him.*
>
> *After he made the crowd go outside, he went into the girl's room and gently took hold of her hand. She immediately stood to her feet! And the news of this incredible miracle spread everywhere* (TPT).

I see two powerful things represented in this story. I believe for many of us our dreams, passions, gifts, and callings have become dormant in our lives. For my mom, she was always told that she was a loser and would never accomplish greatness. When she encountered Jesus, she became alive. How often do we dread Mondays, waiting for the weekend to experience some glimmer of relief from the 9 to 5 jobs that are bogging us down?

We surround ourselves with the hopeless elite. They have huge homes, designer watches, new cars, and are the noisy crowd of mourners who scream from the rooftops, *"Hustle, hustle, make it happen."* Our souls are desperate for life, so we file into church on Sunday and lift our hands for a glimpse of hope. Then we sit quietly in our rows, hoping that a 45-minute message will drown out the week of gossip, complaining, and wailing from our co-workers.

Why is it not working?

I believe the young girl in the story not only represents you and me but the American Church at large. The newspaper headlines proclaim,

"The Church is dead," and from appearances that can seem extremely accurate. Don't get me wrong—the venues on Sunday remain filled, but on Monday we seem to have forgotten all that inspired us just 24 hours earlier.

The time is *now* that Jesus is waking up *His* Church.

When He held the hand of the little girl, it says she immediately "stood to her feet." It is time for the Church, the body of believers, to be *alive, awake,* and *active* in their God-given calling and identity. It's time for the remnant army to stand to their feet! Too many of us are waiting patiently for permission to be the hands and feet of Jesus. When the young girl stood to her feet, we see that the news spread everywhere. Imagine if the Church in America was actively preaching the Gospel in their workplaces, healing people on the subways, releasing freedom during their morning walks, seeing God's redemptive power released regardless of the pain and suffering of their past. This is the good gossip this nation needs!

WE ARE IN REVIVAL

Ring the alarms!

I feel led to say this loud and clear:

We are in revival.

The revival isn't later; *it's now.*

I don't know how to make this any clearer, but we are in a *kairos* moment.

Baptisms are now at the forefront of the Christian event agenda. Churches are meeting and worshiping in parks, beaches, and in parking lots. God's been trying to wake us, shake us, and show us that the things we are earnestly desiring are outside of the four walls of the church.

COVID-19 is the alarm clock we desperately needed.

Saturate was originally intended to be a three-day Christian conference at the Hyatt to equip church attendees to share the Gospel. Ha ha—did you read that? It's hilarious how God is orchestrating events for His glory during *this* moment in history.

Our job is simply to pray and respond.

Too many people are praying *for* revival rather than praying to be *used* by God to revive people. There are times to pray and times to respond. Don't miss revival by praying for revival and refusing to act. We need to do both!

If you are praying for revival and not leaving the prayer closet, *I urge you*—come out! We need you.

A.W. Tozer said it so well when he wrote, "Have you noticed how much praying for revival has been going on of late—and how little revival has resulted? I believe our problem is that we have been trying to substitute praying for obeying; and it simply will not work."[1]

Plane pilot speaker
- elts hot in Colorado do to the smog from the
heat coming from the West.
                        fires in the

Wild fires
                    Revival fires across America
                    end up + down the coast of California.

Where do we go?
What do we do?

        —Take inventory of the prophetic words already
            given.
        Themes / patterns / highlights

5 main things that happen @ Saturate
    1. Wild Worship (prophetic)
    2. Raw Simple Gospel   Sustained through:
    3. Baptism in Water   • Fire groups -discipleship
    4. Baptism in fire   ⟶   • Micro churches
    5. Commission   • local church partners
                                           • # Saturate My City

                Stoke the Flame

Oxygen — Holy Spirit ignites the fire
        * What cities need to be ignited?

HARVESTERS

In John 4:34-38 it is written:

> *"My food," said Jesus, "is to do the will of him who sent me and to finish his work. Don't you have a saying, 'It's still four months until harvest'? I tell you, open your eyes and look at the fields! They are ripe for harvest. Even now the one who reaps draws a wage and harvests a crop for eternal life, so that the sower and the reaper may be glad together. Thus the saying 'One sows and another reaps' is true. I sent you to reap what you have not worked for. Others have done the hard work, and you have reaped the benefits of their labor."*

I find these words to be some of the weightiest in Scripture—also the most ignored.

The reality is, the harvest is ripe *now*.

Jesus Himself is saying that what sustains Him is doing God's will! My question for you is, what is sustaining you? As believers, we love to take a portion of Scripture that comes with a promise of blessing. We will quickly purchase a magnet that says Philippians 1:6, "Being confident of this, that he who began a good work in you will carry it on to completion until the day of Christ Jesus."

Of course, this Scripture is true, as is the whole of Scripture. Yet we feel much more comfortable believing that God is going to carry out completing the good works He started in us and neglect the Scriptures that say, "Hey, you! Yes, you! The one reading this book. The fields are ripe for harvest. Stop looking down, stop waiting for some miraculous sign. This is harvest time! This is the time to reach *souls!*" (Paraphrased from John 4:35.)

I believe the issue for many of us is that we don't need to pray more for the harvest to come, we need to fast and beg God to open our eyes see the harvest that's right in front of us and prevent us from being cowards!

Yet we get stuck. I get it. I am not even close to perfect when it comes to sharing the Gospel. I am like a preschooler learning his or her ABCs when it comes to power evangelism and revival, but at least I am showing up! I think a lot of times we can get wrapped up in methodology. Don't get stuck in, "Should I say this or do that?" God is looking for simple obedience expressed in love.

I believe that in this season, in this *kairos* moment in history, God's way of revival will come through us carrying out the great commission through a simple but faith-filled "yes."

YOU'RE HIRED!

Evangelist D.L. Moody once said, "It is clear you don't like my way of doing evangelism. You raise some good points. Frankly, I sometimes do not like my way of doing evangelism. But I like my way of doing it better than your way of not doing it."

I've always found it quite funny and a bit ironic that there are so many critics online (especially from the church) when it comes to sharing the Gospel. Yes, evangelists are called to preach the Gospel and have a natural, innate ability to do so. Yet the primary role of an evangelist is to equip the saints to preach the Gospel. We see this laid out in Ephesians

4:11. That means that we *all* are called to share the Gospel to our sphere of influence. I encourage you, don't get stuck waiting to have your apologetics and methods all figured out or you'll be waiting a long time.

Our best days of seeing harvest are ahead of us. I believe that our minds cannot even imagine the things that God has in store for the earth. However, we need to lift up our eyes off of ourselves, lay down our way of doing things, and come into alignment with the passions and desires of God.

The best thing we can pray in this season is, *"Lord, what are You doing on the earth right now? What has Your focus and attention? How can I partner with You today? Thank You for taking care of my needs; help me to take care of the needs of others."*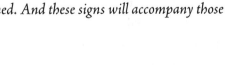

Could we be a generation of people who would say with honesty, *"Not my will, but Your will be done, Lord"*?

Could our hearts' desires be transformed into the desires of God's heart? I believe that God has called you and me to go out and preach the Gospel with power. One of the most empowering Scriptures in the entire Bible comes from the mouth of the resurrected Jesus. I love that Jesus didn't leave His disciples wandering about at a total loss as to what their next steps would be. Jesus said to His disciples in Mark 16:15-17:

> *Go into all the world and preach the gospel to all creation. Whoever believes and is baptized will be saved, but whoever does not believe will be condemned. And these signs will accompany those who believe.*

This is crazy stuff if you read this and believe it! Maybe, just maybe, we don't need another conference on "Identity + Calling."

Imagine if we just put this book down and thought, *Hey, I am going to try that out. If it was good enough for the early disciples, it's good enough for me!* This is *resurrected Jesus* speaking to His *best friends* on earth. He's giving them His best advice on how to live a life full of the Kingdom. He is giving them their new mission, and that same mission is ours today.

Jesus tells *all* of them to *go* and preach the Gospel, to baptize people and make disciples of all the nations. He's like, "Hey besties! I'm giving you the craziest opportunity of a lifetime. You are going to tell people everywhere about Me! I am going to back you up! You won't just see signs and wonders because you went to some event. No way! Signs and wonders will accompany *anyone who believes!* You want to drive out demons—yeah, you can do that in My name!"

I love that Scripture continues on and tells us that the disciples *did* what Jesus said and that the Lord worked with them and confirmed His word with signs. *You want to see healings, miracles, signs, and wonders— preach the Gospel for a year and watch what happens!*

The truth is there is no other major plan God has for you that doesn't include preaching the Gospel and making disciples. This is God's plan through His believers here on the earth. For many of us, we are violently searching for something else and constantly looking inward. Don't believe me? Just type in #Ennegram into Instagram and watch what pops up. There is nothing wrong with discovering more about who you are, but don't allow the enemy to rob you of foundational truths. Perhaps if we come into alignment with God's plan and purpose, we will find our own purpose and our own plans will become clearer.

3/20/17

What's the remnant?
There is purification and refining
Be a part of something greater than ourselves
Not just a service but discipleship
Finding like hearted, like minded people

NOTE

1.   A.W. Tozer, *Prayer: Communing with God in Everything* (Chicago, IL: Moody Publishers, 2016), 47.

CHAPTER 22

The Cost of Revival

As I have said before, I am not a faith healer. I have not been given anything special. What I have is something that any Christian could have if he would pay the price of full surrender and yieldedness. I am absolutely dependent on the mercy of the Lord Jesus Christ.
—Kathryn Kuhlman[1]

The bath was way too hot to get in. I stood vulnerably next to the tub, dipping my toe, only to quickly extract it from the searing heat. I am easily distracted and had let the hot water run in the bath while I paced in the hotel room thinking about the night ahead. I tried to push down on the valve to allow the hot water to drain so I could go in and relax, but as I put my arm back into the burning water, I quickly withdrew it as the water scorched my skin.

I sat on the edge of the tub, closed my eyes, and decided to wait. It was a Saturday night in December, night three of the tent revival, to be precise. Parker and I had checked into one of our favorite "staycation" hotels in Laguna so that we could rest in between sessions and get somewhat of a full night's sleep while Parker's parents stayed overnight with our kids only 20 minutes away. The hotel we booked was a creative refuge for me. The boho decor, Fleetwood Mac spinning on vinyl, a roaring fireplace, and the friendly bartender Frank who brought me bottomless coffee, made for the perfect place to unwind and refresh as we prepared for the tent revival nights.

Parker had already headed out to the field in San Juan Capistrano to meet with the team under the tent. On a recent flight to San Francisco, Parker and I had done a core values assessment. We surprisingly discovered that one of Parker's top five values was "order." The five weeks leading up to the tent revival, Parker had been working through the logistics of getting everything into place, and without him we would have no tent revival to attend.

Between organizing teams, parking, signs, tent logistics, sound, and all of the details that make me feel like I want to cry, we had a space for people to meet God! You see, I am not unorganized. I'm actually quite militant when it comes to administration. However, I also have a highly creative free-flowing side of my personality. The reality for me (and unfortunately it took years to discover this!) is that I can't function in both at the same time. I can organize merchandise, run-sheets, registrations, social media campaigns, budgets—you name it! However, if you ask me to design something, write a message, write a chapter for a book, or share my heart while doing "computer or admin work," it is nearly impossible for me. I am so thankful for how God had orchestrated Parker and me together. I so often get the "credit" for Saturate, but Parker is the backbone to the entire movement. How many times I have cried in his arms as he boldly reminds me of the God I serve!

As I looked out the window and watched the sun setting over Laguna, I realized that time was no longer my friend. I had only about an hour to get ready and prepare my message for the night. Last minute, we decided that I would preach because one of our main speakers was no longer able to join us. I didn't have time to dilly dally and wait for the water to cool off. I took a towel and began to scoop out the water and hurl it at the wall so it would roll down the shower drain nearby. After a few moments of splashing water around the entire bathroom, I was finally able to add a few gallons of cold water to the tub. As I ran my arm under the cold water, I thought about the baptismal pools (or horse troughs) that we had set up next to the tent. The first night, it was about 37 degrees Fahrenheit outside. People were shivering, bundled up under the tent, exposed to the cold December California night.

On Friday night, a handful of people were baptized out of a sheer hunger for God despite the cold. Something was shifting in the tent, but I could feel that the Lord wanted to do more. After the second night, I laid my head on the pillow and heard the Lord say, *"Get ready, you ain't seen nothin' yet."*

To be honest, I dismissed the word, believing that I was just trying to stay positive. The next morning, my friend Tracy, who was home sick, texted me. She prayed for me and encouraged me that God was in our midst. She then said, "Jess, I heard the Lord say, *'Get ready, you ain't seen nothin' yet.'*"

I was in shock.

This moment confirmed to me that the Lord was speaking.

But how, God? What needed to happen? As my fingers danced in the cool water of the bath, I said to God, "I don't think anyone is going to be baptized tonight. It's way too cold outside and the water is freezing."

Then I heard the Lord say to me something that was jolting: "The water is cold, but hell is hot."

I laughed.

I wasn't laughing because hell is hot, but I could kind of just sense an eye roll from God. Like Him saying to me, "C'mon really? They aren't going to get into the water because it's cold? Trust Me, when they know what's at hand, nothing can stop them from getting into that water."

So I slowly closed my eyes, slid into the still very warm bath, and whispered, "Lord, what do You want me to speak about tonight? Please show me. I can't just preach a good message. We need revival!"

WHEN GOD SPEAKS

Earlier that week, I was driving to Anaheim to pick up the merchandise for the night. I am on a group chat with a bunch of Christian women from Orange County who were texting about the Supreme Court hearings regarding COVID-19. I was confused by one of the text messages and decided to call my friend Bev. As I chatted with Bev, she encouraged me about what was ahead for the weekend. Then, almost off the cuff, she said something along the lines of, "Jessi, you are like the woman with the alabaster jar. You have poured it all out to Jesus." Bev is an intercessor, and her words carry so much depth. Her words hit me like an arrow from heaven. Bev and her daughter Lainy are two of the most encouraging and yet fierce women I know. (God will often ignite new things through other burning ones.)

I hung up the phone and opened my Bible. The story of the woman with the alabaster jar is in three of the four Gospels. I love that you can read it from the different perspectives of the eyewitnesses at the table. Though it's a short story, only about seven verses long, God was handing me a "blaze" to revival. I closed my eyes and cried in the car.

LIVE IT TO PREACH IT

Many Christians today have a reputation for being somewhat "hypocritical." To be honest, I don't really blame the media for their criticisms. Celebrity Christian culture has created a platform where if you look right, sound good, and have the right connections you can have an explosive ministry. I've sat in several green rooms as tears streamed down my face after overhearing conversations between speakers that I felt grieved the heart of God. It was like the Wizard of Oz curtain was pulled back.

One of these nights when I was in a green room, I called my sister-in-law Andi who travels and speaks. I was weeping and could barely get the words out: "Andi, I don't know what to do! I can't be here. I hate this. I heard one of the speakers acting so entitled and so mean, and then preaching about humility."

Andi quickly calmed me down and prayed with me. She said, "Jessi, perhaps that is why God has you in there. To bring in something different."

I didn't want that job.

I wanted to be around people far from God.

I wanted to be in nightclubs prophesying to people around bathroom sinks.

Years later, here I was in the tub of our hotel, thinking about the alabaster word Bev had given me two days earlier and realizing I needed to be one who lived the message I preached. I opened up Matthew 26 and began to read it again.

The story opens up like this. Jesus goes to Simon's house. Simon was previously healed of leprosy, which means that he was an outcast in society. I could probably preach an entire message on just that alone. Not only does Jesus heal Simon—which is an incredible miracle!—Jesus also restores Simon. Jesus is headed to the cross, and He is choosing to dine with an outcast. This is the height of His ministry and here He is, about to lay down His life. He can't be found in the green room. No, He is having dinner with the people who need Him the most.

A woman comes into the house, whom many believe is Mary—the same Mary who was delivered from the many demons. This is a woman who was bound and tormented by the enemy. She rushes in. She's not invited. This is very awkward.

It's about to get more awkward. Way more awkward.

She holds up an alabaster jar with expensive perfume, worth about a year's wages. She walks right up to Jesus, pours the oil on His head, then washes His feet with her hair.

We will get into the disciples' reaction in a moment.

However, now, I just want to pause.

As I was reading this story that day, I slowly slid down into the tub and felt the Holy Spirit consume me. Honestly, this moment is hard to describe, but I felt in that tub as if God was giving me a fresh baptism. Preparing me, again, to prepare the way.

I connect on a deep level with John the Baptist. I sometimes feel like a voice crying out in the wilderness, I feel alive outside of the four walls of the church, near the water, baptizing people into a brand-new life. It's near the water that I can see, hear, and press in.

As I thought about this moment with the alabaster jar, a movie scene played before me. I could smell the woodsy perfume fill the room. I watched Mary throw the pottery to the ground. There was no backup plan. A year's wages poured out.

There are times to budget, calculate, and plan. However, when you are face to face with Jesus, we need to have open hands to give it all to Him, however He sees fit. I too was a woman who had been delivered of so many demons. Depression, anxiety, suicidal thoughts, apathy, fear—I can keep going! I remember what it feels like to be far from God. I can't believe that God not only saved me, but He set me free! He continues to set me free and is allowing me to partner with Him in awakening others. The privilege is massive. It's insane. I feel like Simon and Mary all wrapped into one. I was an outcast, I was in rebellion against God, and now He trusts me to lead others to Him and is showing up to the tent revivals we are hosting.

I climbed out of the tub and crawled into bed. I could feel the presence and heat of God all around me. I wondered if I was going to be able to even make it to the event.

I asked God, "What did it feel like for Mary to pour out that jar?" I knew I couldn't preach this message unless I was willing to live it. I thought about the necklace around my neck, a beautiful antique cross that my friend Tami had given me, a treasure. "Lord, did it feel like giving this away?"

I sensed the Holy Spirit telling me to grab random items and put them in my bag. He told me to wear my favorite coat that night and to put blank checks, jewelry, money, and my Bible into my purse. My heart was preparing for what I sensed the Holy Spirit was orchestrating. He was going to ask me to give my things away tonight.

WHAT WOULD THAT FEEL LIKE?

It was about 6:45 p.m. and I jumped into my new Jeep Wrangler and drove quickly to the tent revival site. I drove in silence, as I could feel the weight of what was about to happen. I was already grieving the loss of my jacket and necklace and asked the Lord another question. I said to Him, "A year's wages. That is such a high price. What would that feel like?"

For the last four years, my family had "survived" with one car. Between meetings, travel, and ministry it had become one of the greatest "communication testers" of our marriage. Many early morning conversations began with, "I told you I needed the car."

As I mentioned earlier, God provided for us miraculously when our car died and our house was under construction during the beach revivals. In August, Parker and I sat on a bench and he said, "Jessi, we have enough money for you to put down about half for a car and have small monthly payments. What kind of car do you want?"

I had never been asked that question.

I said to Parker, "I don't know. I don't even know how to think like that. Are you sure it's okay?"

I felt a small orphan mindset slip in. I felt guilty. I thought, *We should probably use this money for something else.* Then I saw a vision of a white Jeep Wrangler with a tan leather interior. I didn't even know if something like this existed! I began to research. I wasn't finding anything remotely close to our budget.

We went to a used car dealership and I drove a beautiful white Jeep Wrangler with black fabric seats. The mileage was high, but it was in our price range. We went to the desk to purchase the car. They showed us the monthly payments, and something looked off. I closed my eyes and asked the Holy Spirit to give me wisdom. Very long story short, they were scamming us over and over again. I kept catching them in one lie after another. We left the used car dealership defeated. I knew I needed to pray and trust God.

Daily, I would check the used car apps on my phone and look at every white Wrangler I could find. After about three weeks, a white Jeep with tan leather interior popped up! The dealership transported it to Costa Mesa, where we lived. I test drove the car with so much excitement. Then we purchased it *that day* and I drove home in my new Jeep. I couldn't believe it!

Now, only a few months later as I pulled into the parking lot of the tent revival site in silence, I felt the Lord say, "Jessi, breaking the alabaster jar would feel like giving up your new Jeep Wrangler."

TESTING THE WORD

I walked up to the tent and saw Parker in the walkway. I pulled him aside and said, "I need to talk to you." He walked over by the porta potty and looked at me with concern. I said, "Parks, I am struggling. I think God is asking me to do something really hard."

I nestled my head into his chest; he pulled me in and said, "Oh babe, what is it?"

I looked up as the lights from the tent lit up his face. I slowly whispered, "I think God wants me to give away my Jeep."

Parker pulled me in and held me as people rushed past us to check in and find a seat. I could hear the roar of the worship team preparing in the background. I wanted to jump into my Jeep and drive away. I wanted to hide.

He whispered into my ear, "Jess, if that's what He is showing you, He will make it clear. If you need to do this, we will be okay. You need to do what God says."

To be honest, I walked away defeated. I was hoping Parker was going to tell me it was a demonic attack. We have a little saying in our house, though: *"The safest place to be is the Kingdom."*

We have a little tester when it comes to hearing God and obedience. If we get a word or feel we hear something from God, we ask ourselves the following questions:

1. Is it scriptural or does it contradict the Word of God?

2. Does it sound like something satan would say?

3. Does it sound like something that is of the flesh?

Sacrificial giving *is* scriptural. Check.

Would satan tell me to give away my Jeep? Perhaps, but in this moment it would glorify Jesus, so probably not.

Does it sound like something that is of the flesh? This question was the sinker. My flesh was crying out, "No!" as I felt the idol of consumerism that plagued Orange County being shredded from my heart. My grip was tight.

As worship began, everyone jumped right in. Something magnetic was happening. The air was shifting. The last two nights we prayed, we prophesied, we believed. Now, something was changing. As everyone danced with joy, I walked over to Joanne, Tami, and Kim. I said, "Ladies, please pray! God's asking me to do something hard. I need a confirmation."

Again, here I was looking for an out.

Friends, this isn't glamorous. I don't know how to communicate this, but we can't just be praying for revival and expect nothing in our lives to change. It's just not like that. God is *God!* And He wants *all* of us.

I paced behind the tent, touching the cold water of the baptismal troughs while praying in tongues.

Pacing.

Pacing.

Pacing.

Then Kim, Joanne, and Tami walked over. They prayed over me and essentially said, "Jessi, God is saying, 'You know what you need to do.'"

I went up to the front to worship. I asked God, "Well, who is the car for?" The last month, I had been thinking nonstop about single moms. About how my mom would ride a bike to work, in the snow, with me strapped on the back. Of course, the car was for one of them.

No.

Matthew 26:8-12 says:

When the disciples saw this, they were offended. "What a total waste!" they grumbled. "We could have sold it for a great deal of money and given it to the poor."

Jesus knew their thoughts and said to them, "Why are you critical of this woman? She has done a beautiful act of kindness for me. You will always have someone poor whom you can help, but you will not always have me. When she poured the fragrant oil over me, she was preparing my body for burial" (TPT).

This radical *generosity* was not for the single moms. This was for Jesus. This was between Him and me. Radical generosity isn't a church or ministry fundraising campaign! Radical generosity is when *you* pay the price to go all in, and when your bank account, your reputation, your life becomes the possession of the Lord.

The cost of living in California is expensive. California is one of the most influential areas in the world—between Hollywood, technology, media, and religion.

If you win California, you can shift a nation.

Revival in California requires more than powerful preaching. It requires a remnant who are totally consumed by God, who have laid down their idols of fame, fortune, and self-idolatry, and who will partner with God "whatever the cost."

God never forces His love upon us.

But He does invite us, all of us, deeper.

I heard the Lord say to me, "Jessi, you can preach a powerful message and many people will get saved and baptized. However, I have heard your cries. I have heard your prayers. If you want revival to open up, the cost is your Jeep."

NOTE

1. Kathryn Kuhlman, *I Believe in Miracles* and "Healing in the Spirit," *Christianity Today*, July 20, 1973.

CHAPTER 23

Radical Revival

The safest place to be is the Kingdom.
—Parker Green

When I heard God tell me that the cost for revival was to surrender my Jeep to Him, I wondered if there could be another way.

Before I stepped on the stage during our tent meeting that night, our friend Mando gave an offering message. It was one of the best offering messages I had ever heard. He asked if we would give God our "blank check." I responded by shouting, "Shut up!" I verbally had to process the shock that I was in! God was confirming to me very loudly the next "blaze" for revival was radical generosity; I had already placed the blank checks in my purse earlier that night! Then my friend Sher shared about the history of California and how the state motto is "Eureka!" During the gold rush, the people paid a high price and gave up everything in hopes of finding riches here. People in California would scream out, "Eureka, I have found what I am looking for." This was another painful confirmation of what God was asking me to do that night.

I stepped onto the stage and the moment felt somber. I felt weight on me, the glory of God. I encouraged the audience to leave, as a warning, because "to whom much is given, much is required." After this moment, they would no longer be able to claim ignorance. They would have to stand before Jesus and He would ask them, "What did you do with what I showed you that night at the tent revival?"

The whole message is online, which you can watch in your spare time. Throughout the message, God was moving in me and through me. It felt like a dance as I heard Holy Spirit telling me to invite Taylor up to play the guitar, bring a bucket of water on the stage, and invite Joel to sit on a chair behind the bucket.

I shared the message of the alabaster jar. I spoke about what happens when we are transformed by Jesus. I shared the Scripture of Matthew 13:44 about how the Kingdom of Heaven is like a treasure in a field. That you may give up everything, but when you do, you get the Kingdom instead.

I knelt down to illustrate the awkwardness of the moment. The radical love that we preach about but so rarely see. I soaked my hair into the tub of water and washed Joel's feet with my hair.

Everyone went silent.

People began to weep and wail and lay down prostrate on the floor.

Something was shifting.

We had a perfect atmosphere for an altar call.

This still wasn't revival.

I took off my coat and had someone give it to one of the single moms in the back. At this point, giving away my coat was easy. This hardly felt like obedience. I then asked Parker to come forward. I handed him our checkbook. I invited every single mom forward. I had Parker write every single mom a check for $100 for each child she had. I shared that this was the role of the Church, to provide and take care of the needs around us. This is not the job of the government; this is our duty.

People began to wail out in repentance. Crying out to God.

I thought, *Just wait. You ain't seen nothin' yet.*

That word God had given me wasn't about some magical fairy dust He was going to sprinkle. He was inviting me to partner with *Him* and to *be* a move of God.

I turned around and Joel was off the stage. I asked him to come back and sit in the chair. I began to cry. I could feel all the stony idols of California being extracted from my heart. I was so upset with myself that this was so hard.

Thank You, Jesus, for loving me so much that You are inviting me deeper into greater purity.

I turned my back toward the crowd and did one last ask to God. "Is there *any other way* to bring revival?"

Then—I saw it.

No one knows about this moment.

This is one of my greatest secrets and treasures.

As I whispered those words, I saw a vision of Jesus in the Garden of Gethsemane.

Matthew 26:36-39 describes the scene:

> *Then Jesus led his disciples to an orchard called "The Oil Press." He told them, "Sit here while I go and pray over there." He took Peter, Jacob, and John with him. However, an intense feeling of great sorrow plunged his soul into deep sorrow and agony. And he said to them, "My heart is overwhelmed and crushed with grief. If feels as though I'm dying. Stay here and keep watch with me."*

*Then he walked a short distance away, and overcome with grief, he threw himself facedown on the ground and prayed, "My Father, **if there us any way you can deliver me from this suffering, please take it from me.** Yet what I want is not important, for I only desire to fulfill your plan for me." Then an angel from heaven appeared to strengthen him* (TPT).

I knew I was no longer in a tent revival.

I was in a holy moment.

We have a saying in our house, *"If you want to do what Jesus did, do what Jesus did."*

I started weeping harder.

Jesus broke His alabaster jar out of His lavish love for us. For Him, the cost was His life. He broke His body for us so that we could be reconciled to the Father. While we rebelled against Him, He died for us to give us *life*.

I felt so embarrassed.

I had been praying and declaring for revival to break out, and when God was asking me to give up a Jeep, it wasn't an immediate "Yes!"

How had I gotten so deceived?

Only ten years ago, I sold everything I had to go on a mission trip for a year to start a relationship with Jesus. Only four years ago, Parker and I quit our full-time jobs and sold nearly everything to come to California.

I was grieved.

I was grieved that in such a short time, the web of what entangles California had secretly entangled me.

I was dying, on stage, for everyone to see.

I was wailing out, shaking, reaching for my keys as quickly as I could.

I then placed the keys to my Jeep into Joel's hand.

I can't believe I had whispered, "Is there any other way?"

Oh Lord, forgive me. Forgive me for tainting those very words that You spoke as You took on my shame and my sin to give me freedom and life. Lord Jesus, forgive us, please forgive us.

"Turn your eyes upon Jesus, look full in His wonderful face, and the things of this world will grow strangely dim, in the light of His glory and grace."

Thank You, Jesus, for trusting me with this.

After this moment of surrender, of breaking my alabaster jar, the Holy Spirit broke out through the tent.

Revival had come again.

People started repenting and being baptized in the cold water.

I went into the tub barefoot, cold, and wet, for two hours, in 34 degrees, and held people as one after another came forward. The fire of God burned within me. As people came out of the water, steam left their body and a cloud of steam filled the area.

A glory cloud of resurrection.

The old gone, the new coming.

God save California.

YOUR ALABASTER JAR

Too many people want the glory and anointing but are not willing to pay the price. What is costly that He is inviting you to pour out at His feet? Mine that day was my Jeep. Another time, it may be something else.

For each one of you reading this, the cost will be different. The cost that this woman poured out upon Jesus was one year's wages. For some of you that $10,000 a year, others $60,000, others $200,000 or more!

Right now, God is asking you to step into the momentum of radical generosity. Though it might not be a year's salary, ask Him to highlight to you one thing that is costly that you can give as an offering unto Him.

There is an exchange that is taking place, right now.

Every area of our lives—nothing is off limits.

For some of you, this is an opportunity to rip out any idols in your heart and lay them at the altar. Some of you need to fast. Some of you need to sell your house. Some of you need to repent of adultery. Some of you need to sign up for a missions trip. Some of you need to lay down your idols of your "passions, dreams, and calling" and start afresh and ask the Lord, "What is Your plan, passion, and dream?"

This is the moment.

Now is the time for radical living.

This is the wildfire.

Your life will never be the same.

CHAPTER 24

If Not Now, Then When?

He wants to breathe fresh anointing on this remnant—not just to be a blessing to those within the four walls of the church, but also to empower believers to be Kingdom ambassadors on the earth. Believers should be so saturated with the Holy Spirit that wherever they go, those they come in contact with are touched by the life-giving power of the Holy Spirit.
—**Tim Sheets**, *Angel Armies*

Right after we had finished the tent revival, we knew we needed a hard rest before the New Year. We work hard, but we rest hard as well. We decided to head to Big Sur during our holiday vacation.

Big Sur is one of my favorite places to "escape" to. As we drove up the windy roads of Pacific Coast Highway along the rocky coastline, I sat back in the passenger seat of Parker's Land Cruiser and played around with the music playlist. I put on "Old Pine" by Ben Howard and looked ahead at the sun rising over the hills and fog-filled raging sea.

The song played quietly in the background as our three children fell asleep for their early morning nap in the back seat.

> *We stood*
> *Steady as the stars in the woods*
> *So happy-hearted*
> *And the warmth rang true inside these bones*
> *As the old pine fell we sang*
> *Just to bless the morning.*
> **—Ben Howard,** *"Old Pine"*

I closed my eyes and could feel the heat from the blazing sun through the window. I could smell the unique fragrance of the central coast, a mixture of pine needles, salty air, and smoky skies. It smelled like adventure; that is simply the only way to describe it.

As our truck swayed from left to right as we followed the coast, I was immediately brought into a vivid vision. It was so clear, like a movie playing before my eyes.

CLOSER

In the vision, I saw a fire raging on a distant hill a few miles ahead.
I could see the smoke filling up the sky.
The fire was full of God's presence and glory.
I saw angels flying in and out of the fire and radiating with color.
As the vision continued, I watched myself run into the fire. My heart beat faster and faster till it beat right out of my chest. Songs drifted in

the air and the feeling of bass filled my bones as the ground shook. I could feel every hindrance burning off of me. In the vision, I watched my former Jeep ignite and blow away in ash. I heard the whispers in my ear of "You are not worthy" and "We are no longer with you" all of a sudden vanish with one whip of the wind, and I immediately felt this deep covering of God's love fall over me: "I love you, I have chosen you, I am with you, I will never leave you." These words sang through my spirit.

Jesus.

All I wanted was Jesus. All I wanted was to be where He was. I knew He was in the fire.

Then, in the vision, I saw camps set up outside of the fire. Preachers, with their charcoaled hands and singed clothes, stood around the tent camps and told powerful stories of what it was like to be in the fire.

A few of the camps packed up their belongings and headed into the fire. They dropped their packs, left their cars, and stepped in boldly. I ran past them, so excited for them to go in and experience the very thing their heart longed for.

A few miles down the road, I saw another camp. The preacher had a few bits of ash on his jacket. He told stories of his experience of being near the fire. People gathered around, leaning in, hanging on his every word and cheering, "More, more, tell us more!" They seemed perfectly content to feel the warmth of the flames, to smell the smoke, but didn't want to go in themselves. They wanted to study the fire from a distance. But that's not what this fire was for.

I ran over and screamed at the top of my lungs, "Get up! Get up! You are so close!"

I knelt down next to a woman on her knees, crying out to God. My filthy, ashy hands grabbed hers and I lifted her up. I said to her, "Come,

come with me! You were not created to hear stories *about* the fire. You are meant to live *in* the fire yourself! Come, come!"

AN INVITATION

Revelation 19:11-16 says:

> *Then I saw heaven opened, and suddenly a white horse appeared. The name of the one riding it was Faithful and True, and with pure righteousness he judges and rides to battle. He wore many regal crowns, **and his eyes were flashing like flames of fire.** He had a secret name inscribed on him that's known only to himself. He wore a robe dipped in blood, and his title is called the Word of God. Following him on white horses were the armies of heaven, wearing white fine linen, pure and bright. A sharp sword came from his mouth with which to conquer the nations, and he will shepherd them with an iron scepter. He will trample out the wine in the winepress of the wrath of God. On his robe and on his thigh he had inscribed a name: King of kings and Lord of lords* (TPT).

God is recruiting His remnant army.

Today.

We have an invitation.

The King of kings and Lord of lords is recruiting the fiery ones. The ones who have counted the cost and say, "Yes, God, I will partner with You, whatever the cost!"

God is inviting us into the fire, because He is the fire.

Hebrews 12:18, 22, 26-29 says:

> *You have not come to a mountain that can be touched and that is burning with fire...But you have come to Mount Zion, to the city of the living God, the heavenly Jerusalem. ...At that time his voice shook the earth, but now he has promised, "Once more I will shake not only the earth but also the heavens." The words "once more" indicate the removing of what can be shaken—that is, created things—so that what cannot be shaken may remain. Therefore, since we are receiving a kingdom that cannot be shaken, let us be thankful, and so worship God acceptably with reverence and awe, for our "God is a consuming fire."*

THIS ISN'T ABOUT REVIVAL

At this point, I hate to break it to you, but this book isn't about revival. Oh gosh, I beg God to forgive me if you have gotten this far and you think I am going to give you five steps to hosting a tent meeting, or gather a crowd on a beach, or share the Gospel in a grocery store.

This isn't about ministry.

This isn't about a movement.

This is about Jesus.

This is about Emmanuel—God with us.

My friends, my kin, my fellow voyagers on the windy road, refusing to settle in at camp, pressing on, with bloody toes and a wild heart. To those who have resolved that they "are all in."

Keep going. We must link arms and keep going.

We each have a part to play, no part more or less significant. Let the apostle plant churches, let the evangelist train us to win souls, let the mother disciple the next generation, let the financial investor multiply resources and invest into the Kingdom and train us all in generosity! Let us all prophesy. Let us all dream dreams. Let us all not grow weary!

That great cloud of witnesses—Charles Finney, A.W. Tozer, Paul the apostle, Aimee Semple McPherson, Reinhard Bonnke, Billy Graham—they are cheering us on and passing the baton to us! What a privilege! They are saying, *"Don't give up now! This is the hour!"* You see, this matter of revival is a race marked out for you and me!

Hebrews 12:1-2 says:

> *Therefore, since we are surrounded by such a great cloud of witnesses, let us throw off everything that hinders and the sin that so easily entangles. And let us run with perseverance the race marked out for us, fixing our eyes on Jesus, the pioneer and perfecter of faith.*

Let's violently throw off all that hinders and entangles us. Oh, how the enemy has used all his same old tricks to keep us distracted. It's time to shake it off and run! It's all about Jesus. Fix your eyes on the burning one, allow His flames to consume every part of your being, and let's burn, burn, burn!

NOW

I hope by now you can feel the presence of the living God calling you in, whispering to you, "It's time."

In 2020, I was baptized *three* times.

Each moment was an invitation from my Creator to drown the former things and to go all in with what He had in store for me.

He is calling you in, into the waters, into the fire.

As a prophetic act of drowning your old way of living, your thoughts that wander to and fro, and as a sign for you being willing to yield it all—if today you want to be a living sacrifice, a burning one on the altar of the living God—whether this is your first time or hundredth time...

I want to invite you to fill up a bathtub, go the ocean, visit a lake, take a bottle of water, or do whatever you need to do and...

Be baptized.

When you come out of the water, I want you to place your hand over your heart and read these words aloud over yourself:

Fasten me upon your heart as a seal of fire forevermore.

This living, consuming flame

will seal you as my prisoner of love.

My passion is stronger

than the chains of death and the grave,

all consuming as the very flashes of fire

from the burning heart of God.

Place this fierce, unrelenting fire over your entire being.

Rivers of pain and persecution

will never extinguish this flame.

Endless floods will be unable

to quench this raging fire that burns within you.

Everything will be consumed.

It will stop at nothing

as you yield everything to this furious fire

until it won't even seem to you like a sacrifice anymore
(Song of Songs 8:6-7 TPT).

*Holy Spirit, as an act of faith, I bless the person holding this book in their hands. I baptize them now **to be born again**, in the power of the Holy Spirit! Fill them with **power**, Lord. Burn away every entanglement in the world. Revive them, give them creative ideas, and let them be a wildfire of Your love, here on earth. **Raise them up, as a part of Your remnant army, to ignite their city with Your fire and love**. Amen.*

Song of Solomon — 8:6-7

Fasten me upon your heart as a (seal)
on fire forevermore
This living consuming flame will seal you
as my prisoner of love
My passion is stronger than the chains of
death & the grave
all consuming as the very
flashes of fire
from the burning heart of God

Place this FIERCE
unrelenting fire over your
(entire) being
Rivers of pain & persecution
will never extinguish this flame.
Endless floods will be unable to quench
this raging fire that burns within
you.

Everything will be consumed
It will stop at (nothing)
as you yield (everything) to this furious fire
until it won't even seem to you
like a sacrifice

anymore.

Acknowledgments

To burn and ignite others with the fire, power, and love of Jesus. Gosh, that is all I want to do on this earth. This message has been developing in me since that cold night in my tiny Manhattan apartment. There are so many people who have shaped me and pushed me to go *all in* as a radical follower of Jesus!

As I have penned my soul unto pages, there are so many who have cheered and believed in this message for this hour. Parker, honestly, I am obsessed with you. You are the strongest, most loving, disciplined, and supportive man I know. I can't imagine being married to anyone else. Thank you for showing me how to radically obey Jesus and for believing in every crazy idea I come out of the shower with. Your steadfastness and stability have covered me so that I can live as "Jessi fully alive!" Also, thank you for believing that I was the "best preacher" before I ever preached, haha!

My three wild ones, David, Ethan, and Summer. My greatest honor is to create a small path into the fire for you to follow. I pray that His Word would be a lamp unto your feet and that you would live a life in revival that never ends. I love you, all the time.

Mom, honestly, there would be no *Wildfires* book and no Saturate beach and tent revivals without your sacrifice. Thank you for putting a stake in the ground for our family. Thank you for playing Keith Green in the house when I would complain, for dragging me to church, for crying when you read the Bible, and all the other ways you embarrassed me as a teenager. When death was on my doorstep, thank you for your patience. For showing me the greatest example of evangelism and leading me into the love of Jesus. Dad, thank you for redeeming what a father is and showing me more about the Father's love. For the ways you would allow me to verbally process my thoughts, for reading my writing in high school, and for believing in my dream to communicate with passion to others. Jackie, thank you for being an incredible little sister and for always keeping things real and keeping me humble. ;)

I wrote a book! A dream of a six-year-old girl has happened! Thank you, thank you, thank you to the entire Destiny Image team. Honestly, I can't imagine trying to write this book without such a Spirit-led group. Larry Sparks, I don't even know what to say. Thank you for the way that you burn for Jesus, for the passion you have for revival, and for the friendship you have given to Parker and me. Thank you for coming to that hole-in-the-wall restaurant in Huntington Beach to seek out a possible revivalist! Thank you for saying "Yes!" to this book when it was just a phone call about an idea God dropped into me. Tina and Ryan Pugh, I can't believe you guys are real people! Thank you for inviting Parker and me to be raw and transparent with you without an ounce of judgment, but instead you poured out oceans of love, prophetic words, and continued encouragement. Thank you for helping us navigate leading, writing, and offending (whoops!) so many! Jen Miskov, thank you for editing my book. I still can't believe that I have the honor of having my favorite revival historian to be my editor and my close friend! Thank you for the long, long, longgggggggg (haha, I can do things like that in this section!) hours of editing in my RV, for helping me rework, rewrite, cut out, refine, and define my words over, and over, and over again! Thank you for reminding me 1,000 times this past year that I am not crazy, I am not alone, and that what we were experiencing was "normal" revival stuff! Also, thanks for not making me cut out The Chainsmokers lyrics despite your suggestions. ;) John and Tammy you guys are the quickest production managers and editors in the world! I guess, kinda, thank you for editing so fast and giving me short deadlines to get this book into the hands of future revivalists ASAP! Shaun, thank you for helping us launch The Remnant Rising Podcast and amplifying our message in this season. Christian, sorry for the 100 "inspo" photos for my cover. Thank you for having a value for branding and for making my *dream* cover a reality. Somehow, you managed the impossible—a book called *Wildfires* without a cover full of flames! Haha, we did it!

Gracie, Leah, and Trish, thank you for being real best friends. Despite my inability to pick up a phone, you have not given up on me! For real, thank you for the billion tough conversations that have refined me. Thank you for celebrating victories when I don't know how. Thank you for allowing me to just be me. Montauk adventures, fancy brunches, creative conversations, bad relationships, false prophets, and "fully alive" moments—thank you.

Taylor, Vic, Kendra, and Kendall—one of my greatest accomplishments is leading the four of you. Thank you for taking discipleship seriously, for pressing into the hard conversations, for living radically and being the most fun. Whether we are playing Nertz (or I'm crushing you at Avalon) or we are baptizing people in troughs or demon-possessed people are throwing oxygen tanks at us, I am thankful that the Lord has entrusted me to lead you four on the journey into the fire and it is my *honor* to watch you each *burn* in such unique ways that are catalytic to this nation! Let's go!

Bob and Mavis (Dad and Mom), thank you for being the best in-laws in the entire universe! Your love for people convicts me and challenges me to pause, press in, and allow myself to risk being hurt for the sake of the Gospel. Thank you for the many ways you have sacrificed. Thank you for raising up my husband to be a man of honor. Thank you for leaving everything to pioneer and plant churches in California. Thank you for watching my babies and loving them well so Parker and I can lead revival. Thank you for loving me when I was just a broken girl, sitting on your couch, wondering if I'd ever get married and if I'd ever be used by God.

Andi, sis, I just really miss you to the core. I miss brainstorming ways to catalyze movement with you. Thank you for pushing me to live a holy, consecrated life. Thank you for teaching me how to prepare messages, navigate green rooms without crying, and being a powerhouse example of a woman who can preach. Thank you for encouraging me to reach the lost (you are the first person I ever told I was an evangelist), and thank you for making Christianity uncomplicated!

Joanne and Tracy, thank you for opening up your arms and your life when I was the "newbie" in Orange County. Thank you for the late-night prayers, the million text messages, and the real conversations to keep my heart soft and be transparent. Thank you for lifting my arms when I wanted to quit so many times. Chris, Sher, Tami, Kim, Cathy, Bev, Lainy, Lauren, Caitlin, Patti, Kahanah, Amanda, Sophie, Diane—you ladies are the burning ones who have prepared the altar in Orange County! Cathy, thank you for being obedient to the Lord and connecting me based on a prophetic word! Tami and Bev, thank you for sacrificing so much time and being so diligent to gather the women and create a space for the Holy Spirit and fun! I absolutely *could not* have done Saturate without you all. Thank you for not just praying for revival but living revival!

Doug and Debbie Healy, Kris Kildosher, Paula Dievendorf, Theresa and Kevin Dedmon, Joe Ferguson, Mando Matthews, Hastings, Theobalds, Shambrooks, Blues, Melody, Tim Manigault, Tommy Murphy, Elizabeth Tiam-Fook, Joel Mott, Ben and Jodie Hughes, Ana Werner—

thank you for saying "Yes!" Thank you for partnering with us when so many things were just visions. Thank you for standing with us against opposition. Thank you for sacrificing your time, your gifts, and for pressing in for revival in California and beyond when everyone said "Cancel!" Thank you for your prayers and for just loving us well and linking arms with us in various seasons.

Thank you, Reinhard Bonnke, Charles G. Finney, and A.W. Tozer. Thank you for igniting the fire for revival within me. Thank you for fathering me in dreaming bigger with God, overcoming opposition, and living a lifestyle of risk. Thank you for creating a path for my generation to walk in! I can't wait to celebrate all of the victory with you in heaven!

Bill Johnson and Heidi Baker, hi. You don't know me (yet), but I had to acknowledge you both in this book. From a distance, thank you for leading me into the depths of intimacy with Jesus from which I have never recovered. Through your messages and books, you have taught me how to be filled with the Holy Spirit, how to live a life of revival and stop for the one. I can't wait to sit on a couch one day with you both and cry as we witness the salvation of America in our lifetime.

Lastly, thank You, Jesus. Thank You for being my best friend. Thank You for rescuing me when I was so far from You and pouring out Your love on my bleeding heart. This is all for You. I hope You love my book and are so proud of me, and I pray that everyone who reads it can know You like I do!

About Jessi Green

Jessi Green is a revivalist, full-time missionary, director of Saturate OC, and co-lead pastor of Salt Churches alongside her husband, Parker.

After being radically saved in her Manhattan apartment after an encounter with God, she has been on a journey to go "all in" and discover the "real" Jesus and ignite the Church.

She is passionate about preaching the Gospel, shaking religious systems, and equipping the saints to make disciples. She believes that everyone is qualified to share the Good News and teach others to follow Jesus. While enjoying the sun in California with her two sons David Leonidas and Ethan Everest and baby daughter Summer Kingsley, she passionately speaks about what it means to follow a Jesus who is *alive* and wants to transform cities and *your life!*

If you would like to invite Jessi to speak or to find messages, tools, and resources please visit JessiGreen.com.

Say hi on Instagram @Jessi.Green

Experience a personal revival!

Spirit-empowered content from today's top Christian authors delivered directly to your inbox.

Join today!
lovetoreadclub.com

Inspiring Articles
Powerful Video Teaching
Resources for Revival

Get all of this and so much more, e-mailed to you twice weekly!

LOVE TO READ CLUB
by **D** DESTINY IMAGE